The Strings
of My
Heart

Beatrice Garcia

Psalm 71:17 – 19

Since my youth, O God You have taught me,
And to this day I declare your marvelous deeds.
Even when I am old and gray
Do not forsake me, O God,
Till I declare your power to the next generation,
Your might to all who are to come.
Your righteousness reaches to the skies, O God,
You who have done great things.
Who, O God, is like you?

My Life's Story

The Strings
of My
Heart

Beatrice Garcia

WestBow
PRESS
A DIVISION OF THOMAS NELSON

WestBow Press books may be ordered through booksellers or by contacting:

WestBow Press
A Division of Thomas Nelson
1663 Liberty Drive
Bloomington, IN 47403
www.westbowpress.com
1-(866) 928-1240

ISBN: 978-1-4497-5465-5 (e)
ISBN: 978-1-4497-5464-8 (sc)
ISBN: 978-1-4497-5466-2 (hc)

Library of Congress Control Number: 2012909575

Printed in the United States of America

WestBow Press rev. date: 7/02/2012

To my beloved family and friends
And to all those
Who will get to know me
Through the reading of this book

Table of Contents

Foreword

How This Book Came to Be

When the idea for this project first came up, it seemed like a simple matter. It would be fun to gather all of Mom's interesting stories that she had already written and put them together in some type of chronological order. There were just a few which needed to be translated from Spanish into English, and then they could all be put into one document. I knew that if I added to her stories she would make sure the result was absolutely factual, thanks to her clarity of mind and amazing memory at age ninety-five. At one point, after asking Mom questions regarding each story, it was clear that there was still more that needed to be added and more new stories that needed to be written.

My sister, Alice and I decided to work together on this project and we started filling in the gaps. It was like putting together a big puzzle and each piece was making this memoir a more beautiful and complete representation of a precious life. As we wove each new story into those she had already written, we could see the significant threads that ran from beginning to end. Together these stories created a unique tapestry, a splendid weaving with a unifying theme. It recorded the irrefutable and undeniable fact that an invisible presence had directed every step, every trial, and every triumph of her life.

As we are approaching the final draft of Mother's book, I think about all the different directions her life may have taken had her aspirations been different. She had many opportunities and options. For example, had her goal been wealth and security, she might have at age fifteen married Ezzel and become part owner of a canning factory. If she had coveted an inheritance, she might have told the attorney that her deceased father had provided child support for her when he was alive, and walked away with thousands of dollars during a time of economic depression. Had she chosen to repay grief for grief, she might have chosen to sue the young man that accidentally killed her two precious sons. What if she had demanded that her boss leave her part of the business when he retired as he had promised? The "What ifs" are endless and their outcomes unpredictable, but her choices were consistent with a woman of virtue. She was not living in this world to gain earthly riches. She was living here to make others rich in faith and in Christ's love.

In bringing all these stories together, we were able to see the threads that run through her life joining all the events together and revealing the wonderful way that a sovereign Lord chooses and predestinates and calls. Mother heard the call. As a young child, she heard about Jesus through songs and the messages of a dear aunt and grandmother who were faithful to proclaim and live the message of a risen Savior; the message that tells a young fatherless girl that there is a heavenly Father that loves her with an unfailing, everlasting love. Mother believed in that love at a young age; she craved it, she sought it, she pursued it, she embraced it, and she gained it! She left many things behind to go wherever the Lord led her. She believes that whatever promises the heavenly Father has given us in His Word, He will fulfill.

While the task of putting this book together has been a much greater endeavor than we had envisioned, it has nevertheless, been a great privilege and pleasure. Mother has chosen to pursue the greatest reward – to live a life without offense toward God or man. She looks forward to a glorious promise given not only to her but also to everyone who loves the Lord and is waiting for the appearing of Him in His Kingdom.

Elizabeth Martin (Daughter of Beatrice Garcia)

Preface

The journey of my life has been interesting and I pray that this book will inspire the reader to trust in Christ, no matter what circumstances life may bring them. It has been said that I am a member of "The Greatest Generation" and that may be so. I have lived through World War I, The Spanish Flu, The Great Depression and World War II. But I believe "The Greatest Generation" is the one that hears God's voice and obeys. I pray that the readers of this book may listen for that calling in their life and fulfill their destiny.

I thank God for this wonderful life, and I hope that my descendants and you will enjoy this book of memories. May the Lord Jesus bless my humble writing.

So I Will Write

By Beatrice Garcia

I write to tell my history,
Removing any mystery.
Nine decades have flown by,
The adage doesn't lie.

The stories I love so well,
I feel the need to tell.
So I must start to write,
My children to delight.

They will know my life,
My sadness, trials and strife.
My youth and happy marriage,
How I wheeled their baby carriage.

Yes, I taught them how to pray
And read the Bible every day.
This gift I gave them from the start,
To love the Lord with all their heart.

Life moves too fast a pace today,
Families don't talk; live far away.
Computers replacing conversations,
About the beauty of God's creation.

There's not much left for me to fix,
Now I'm approaching ninety-six.
Thank God, my mind, is nice and clear,
So please sit down, my story to hear.

Acknowledgments

I want to express my gratitude to those who helped me write my life story. First I want to acknowledge my late husband, Patricio Garcia who took me to journalism classes at the Montebello Senior Center when I was in my early seventies. My husband and I were inseparable throughout our long marriage, so his story is included in mine. It was at the Senior Center that I first started writing my autobiographical memories. I want to acknowledge my son, Ruben who encouraged me to continue writing. I appreciate the labor of my daughters, Elizabeth Martin and Alice Landeros, who compiled and organized my stories and gathered the pictures that give more life to these pages. I continued to tell them events of my life to help fill in the gaps that I can still remember clearly at ninety-six years of age. They labored tirelessly to make this book attractive, and an accurate account of my life; they are my co-authors.

A dear friend and neighbor heard about our project and early on volunteered to proofread the manuscript as we developed it. Stephanie Leon, an English major, teacher and writer, willingly and freely rendered her services. She provided us with excellent feedback and recommendations. She encouraged us to continue adding all the stories that I could still remember, and so my book grew to be larger than originally planned. With her help and that of other final reviewers, we were able to make it what it has become – a polished well-written story. In addition I want to thank my friend Pat Reeve who prayed with me that the Lord would help me complete this project – which He did. We thank you dear friends for your labor and prayers.

Beatrice Garcia

PART ONE

*Jesus swept across these broken strings
and now I sing again.*

Chapter 1

The Rio Grande Valley

Before I formed you in the womb I knew you,
before you were born I set you apart.

JEREMIAH 1:5

I t was the 1900s and the turn of a new century. My grandparents, Benjamin Cantu and Severa Rodriguez Cantu, were raising their children in the small town of Los Aldamas, Nuevo Leon, Mexico. My grandmother, Mama Severita, as we lovingly called her, wanted all her children to receive a formal education since she had not. During that period, most girls stayed at home to help with the domestic duties and did not go to school. It was a time of revolution in Mexico, and schools were often shut down. In spite of this, God answered my grandmother's wish. A Methodist minister named Florencio Toscano opened a private Christian school near their home in Los Aldamas. Señor Toscano instructed her children in reading, writing, and arithmetic. He also began to teach them the Word of God. This was a real blessing. In that town, very few knew how to read, and most did not own a Bible. The Bible was read in the Catholic Church, but only in Latin, a language the people did not understand.

The civil unrest in Mexico was frightful. Mother told me stories of how Grandmother would take the children out to sleep in the cornfield if they heard the rebels were in town. The rebels were abusive, often forcing the young men to join them and frequently taking advantage of the women. Thank God that neither my mother's family nor their home was ever raided. The Mexican Revolution helped my grandparents make the decision to pack everyone up and migrate to the United States to a region known as "The Rio Grande Valley."

Once in the United States, my grandparents came to a small town in southern Texas named Chapin, which was just beginning to grow. The name of the town was later changed to Edinburg. Here, my grandparents and some of the older children found jobs clearing the land for the city in preparation for the construction of new buildings. The family cut down trees, cleared the fields, and set up temporary living quarters in tents while they worked the land. After earning enough money, my grandparents packed up and moved to Mission, just a few miles from Edinburg, where they purchased a home and settled down. My grandparent's home was on the corner of 2nd and Oblate Avenue in Mission, Texas.

I was born at 7:30 in the morning on April 27, 1914, in my grandparents' home. Everyone had left early to work in the fields before it got too hot. My mother was home alone and started to feel some contractions. She went across the street to visit Michaela Gutierrez, a midwife and also one of my father's relatives. I came into this world two months ahead of schedule. Michaela guessed I weighed about five pounds. My grandmother named me Beatrice after a close friend and a popular novel of the time, *Beatrice and Dora.* Mother said I hardly had any hair and looked more like a Gutierrez than a Cantu. I was christened in May of 1914, and my godparents were Francisca Gutierrez (my father's first cousin) and her son Victor Gutierrez.

My mother was Paula Cantu, the fourth of thirteen children born to Benjamin and Severa Cantu. My father was Graciano Gutierrez, the son of Bartolo Gutierrez and Tomasa Ochoa (of Spanish descent). Graciano owned and ran a small neighborhood grocery store near my mother's home. Mother would go to this store to buy groceries. That is how they met and how their courtship began. My father was thirty-seven years old, and my mother was only seventeen when they married. I heard that my parents had a beautiful wedding at the Catholic Church in Mission on June 1, 1913 and that my paternal grandmother helped with the wedding expenses. However, my mother was not ready to give up all the joys of being eighteen to be a stay-at-home housewife. They separated two months before I was born. I was not told why my parents' marriage failed, so I can only guess based on the very little I learned as a child. I assume that the age difference was a major issue. My mother returned to her parents' home. They received her on the condition that she would never go back to my father again. She complied, and this is how the story of an absent father began in my life.

Mother managed to save up enough money by ironing clothes for a neighbor to buy a baby carriage that served as my cradle. As was customary in those days, women did not work for forty days after the birth of a child. Since she was single, however, Mother returned to work much sooner. She left me and my bottle with my grandmother and my aunts. I was told that on her first day back to work, I refused to drink from the bottle. One of my aunts felt sorry for me and decided to push me in my carriage to where Mother was working. She would take a break from her ironing and breast-feed me daily. This became the routine. Since I did not like a baby bottle, I learned to drink out of a cup as soon as I could grab on to things.

When I was around eight months old, my Uncle Librado's wife, Jesusita, would rock me in her arms before putting me to bed in my cradle. She would sing a lullaby that said, *"Duermase, mi niña"* (Go to sleep, my baby).

One night, to her surprise, I responded by saying, "Eh-me ceh-te."

"Listen to this child," she told her husband, "Beatrice is already saying the alphabet."

"She's not saying the alphabet," he told her, "she is saying 'you go to sleep.'" *Duermase usted* were my first words.

One evening, when I was a year and a half old, my Aunt Jesusita was trying to put me to sleep. Apparently, I was not sleepy and wanted to stay up with the rest of the family. Seeing my resistance, she told me that if I didn't go to sleep, the coyote would come get me.

According to Aunt Jesusita, at that moment, I pointed out the window and said to her, "Look, here he comes now!" They all got a laugh at my response. Even at this young age, it appears that I understood they were joking with me, and I enjoyed joining in on their storytelling and making everyone laugh.

When I outgrew the cradle, I began sleeping in my mother's bed. After Mother re-married, that carriage cradled my half sister Theodora, who was born in Mexico. When I was about seven years old, my mother gave the carriage away. I was sad to see it leave our house. I have fond memories of that baby carriage and can still picture it clearly in my mind.

Chapter 2

Patent Leather Shoes

Seek first the kingdom of God and his
righteousness, and all these things shall be
added unto you.

MATTHEW 6:33

Soon after I was born, World War I began. A few years later, the
United States got involved. My grandmother, fearing her older
sons might be drafted by the Army, urged Papa Benjamin to move
us all back to Mexico. We moved to Los Olmos, a ranch just outside
of General Bravo. There we enjoyed a quiet and peaceful life in the
country. We ate chickens and had fresh eggs and milk every day.
The family also grew corn, squash, pumpkins, and beans. I was very
happy living with my mother, my young aunts and uncles, and my
grandparents in Mexico.

The date was September 27, 1917. I remember every detail of that day
so well: bouquets of fragrant roses, guests arriving in horse-drawn

carriages, and everyone in his or her best clothes. They greeted each other warmly. The air was humming with excitement.

In the backyard, my uncles cooked meat on a grill. The patio had large tables with nice white linen tablecloths. My Aunts Severa and Adela were setting the tables with china and pretty glasses. My best friend, Gertrude, shouted, "Beatrice, want to come to my house and see my new kittens?" I didn't want to go anywhere; I wanted to know what was going on. There was going to be a big party and no one had told me anything. Surely, something very special was going to happen. Aunt Adela dressed me in a new pink dress and the beautiful black patent leather shoes that Mother had bought me, but not allowed me to wear. I usually went around barefoot, so I eagerly waited for the day I could wear my shoes. That day had finally arrived.

Gertrude and I had been outside playing and after a while, I decided to go into the house. I saw a man standing at the door who apparently was an usher. I sneaked past him looking for my mother and I saw her at the far end of the room. She was dressed in a beautiful long pink dress, a pretty white hat, and white gloves. She looked so beautiful, but why was she ignoring me? Then I saw, for the first time, the handsome stranger holding my mother's hand. I had walked right into my mother's wedding ceremony.

I started running toward my mother, right in the middle of their vows, but someone scooped me up into her arms. I began to scream loudly and felt that my heart would break. My Aunt Adela carried me outside. She held me in her arms and comforted me with a kiss. We heard the musicians start to play and she took me outside to hear the music.

Two men were playing guitars and another man, an accordion. I stopped sobbing, but I wanted my mother. Then Aunt Severita came and took me in her arms and explained that today Mama Paula got married to Jesús Rutoskey so he was now my new father and now the three of us would live together. I did not want to leave my grandparents and I did not want a new father. How could this stranger be my father? Yet, no one had asked my opinion.

Jesús Rutoskey was of Polish descent. He was a friend of Lupe Leal Arizpe, and her husband. Lupe was my mother's best friend. Mother would often visit them and that was how she met Jesús. He was a widower who had lost both his wife and child. Lupe, thinking that they would make a good couple, encouraged the courtship. He was about ten years older than my mother.

After my mother had married Jesús, we moved into his cabin in General Bravo. There was no real reason for me to dislike him, since he was always kind to me. All I knew was that someone had suddenly come into my life, and between my mother and me. How could she love this stranger as much as she loved me? My mother would ask me if I still loved her. I would answer that I loved her, but I did not like Jesús.

My new stepfather had an interesting heritage. The story was passed down by my great-grandfather Luz Cantu and went like this: The French Emperor Napoleon III invaded Mexico and wanted to establish French governmental rule. Benito Juarez, the first full-blooded indigenous national ever to serve as President of Mexico, courageously resisted the French occupation, refusing to accept a government "imposed by foreigners," and Mexico went to war. France brought soldiers from other European nations.

Mariano Rutoskey Tradoskey was one of those soldiers. Mariano was thirteen years old, and the youngest of three brothers. His two older brothers were killed in battle, and the Mexican Army took Mariano prisoner. One day, the captain gave orders to his soldiers to kill all the prisoners. My great-grandfather, Luz Cantu, who was one of the Mexican soldiers, took Mariano aside and said, "I will take care of this one." He marched Mariano into the woods and pulled out his musket. He told Mariano, "Run quickly and quietly. I am going to shoot, but not at you. Run for your life!" Mexico won an initial victory over the French in Puebla, Cinco de Mayo (May 5), 1862.

Luz Cantu told this story to his sons, including my grandfather, Papa Benjamin. He told them that he could not find it in his heart to kill such a handsome youth. After escaping, Mariano found work as a farmhand. He later married and had five children, three sons and two daughters. One of Mariano's three sons was Jesús Rutoskey. The boy my great-grandfather had spared, Mariano, fathered a son who married my mother. This was my new stepfather. We have recently discovered that this kind man was a Polish Jew.

Jesús owned a large property with two small cabins. One cabin was for cooking and eating and the other served as both living room and bedroom. In the back yard were many mesquite trees and a small brook. When it rained, the water in the brook came from the nearby hills and fed into the San Juan River. Sometime after their marriage, they hired some workers to build a new house on the property. The house was built several years later, but I never lived in it. The new house was made of eighteen-inch stone blocks. It didn't have electricity or plumbing and the bathroom (or outhouse) was a good distance from the main house.

My mother and stepfather lived in that house all their married life. My stepfather died at age ninety-four and my mother continued living in that house until her passing at age ninety-six. As far as I know, the house is still standing. As a married adult, I faithfully sent a portion of my income to my mother for her support. I continued to do this for as long as she lived. With this money, she was able to gradually add electricity, plumbing, and a telephone line. She also bought kitchen appliances that made her domestic chores easier. Some years later, she added another room to the house which she was able to rent out.

Jesús and my mother were always busy on the farm. They had a small herd of cows which they milked every morning. Some of the milk was for us, and some was sold to the neighbors. Mother also made cheese and butter, and I always drank the buttermilk left after the butter had been churned. Whatever milk remained was boiled so it wouldn't sour. When this work was done, my stepfather meticulously washed all the milk buckets and cheese cloths. Finally, it was time to take the cows and sheep down to the pasture which was on the other side of the river. We took the sheep dogs with us to keep the livestock from straying. My mother and I had a tradition that I enjoyed. While Jesús was busy tending the cows, Mother and I would bathe in the river. She was a very good swimmer, and as soon as we reached the river, she would dive in and swim across. Since I was just a pre-schooler and I didn't know how to swim, I would nervously watch from the riverbank. She would comfort me by saying, "Don't worry, I won't drown." After our bath, we would dry and put on our clean clothes. We would wash our old clothes in the river and then hang them on the bushes to dry. In the evening after returning home, Jesús would feed the cows nopales (cactus) that he had scorched in the fire to remove the thorns. The trip to the river was always a special treat for me.

Mother used to love to teach me poems in Spanish. When I was about four years old, she would take me to the general store, lift me on to the counter, and ask me to recite the poems to all the customers. Mother had shown me how to dramatize the poem with facial expressions and hand gestures which I did with much enthusiasm. How I loved to perform the beautiful poems my mother had taught me! My favorite poem to recite was *El Caracol*. The storeowner loved to hear me and when I was done reciting, he would gift me with a piece of candy.

I remember how industrious my mother was. She knew how to sew men's shirts, roll cigarettes, and make cheese and butter. When she would go out to sell her goods, she would leave me home alone to take care of myself. I found things to do. I didn't have toys and gadgets like kids have today, so I used my imagination and creativity instead. I would find pieces of broken china and use them as my toy dishes. I would make a table using corncobs for table legs and a piece of cardboard for a tabletop. I learned how to make my own rag dolls, and they would join me at my tea parties. Sometimes I played with my two neighbor friends, Evangelina and Maria, or my step-cousins Concha and Cipriana, who lived next door. When no one was around to play with me, I would talk to my beautiful cat, Blanca Nieve (Snow White).

When World War I ended, the warring nations signed a peace treaty on November 11, 1918, which became known as Armistice Day. That day, the *New York Times* reported the following:

"They stopped fighting at 11 o'clock this morning. In a twinkling, four years of killing and massacre stopped as if God had swept His omnipotent finger across the scene of world carnage and cried, 'Enough'."

After the war, my grandparents and their children returned to Texas once again. In search of employment, they moved several times. They lived in Harlingen, then moved to Mission, and finally settled in the small town of Donna. I was sad when they returned to Texas, because this time I had to stay in Mexico with my mother and new stepfather.

Although the war was over, people were still dying of what was called the "Spanish Flu." An estimated fifty to one hundred million people were killed by this influenza. In the United States, it was reported that there were ten times more people dying of the flu than there were dying in the battlefields of World War I. The Spanish Flu continued spreading around the world since the returning soldiers brought the disease home with them. Even in our small hometown in Mexico, we did not escape this contagious disease. My mother, who was now expecting her first (and only) child by my stepfather, Jesus, came down with it, and I contracted it from her. Because my mother could not care for me, they took me over to Ana Rutoskey's house, since I too was burning up with fever. I heard a lady who was attending me that day say, "This child has not eaten for three days, and she's going to die!" Then another lady said, "Let her die. Her mother is dying also. Who will care for the child if she lives?" At that age, I did not know what it meant, "to die," so I was not afraid. Yet, God's will was that I not die, and neither did my mother. It was not until later that I realized that my encounter with the deadly Spanish Flu was the first time God had spared my life. In December, my little sister was born. They named her Dora, but my stepfather changed it to Theodora after his mother. She was fair, with dark eyes and black hair, but most importantly, she was healthy.

The year was 1919 and I was five years old. On this particular day, which happened to be a beautiful summer morning, I was very excited. We woke up very early and got dressed in our nice clothes and shoes. We were going on a short trip to visit my beloved grandparents and my aunts and uncles who lived in the United States. The day I had been waiting for had finally come. My mother said good-bye to my stepfather just as the horse-drawn buggy arrived. The driver helped me into the carriage and placed our valise on the floor at my feet. My mother climbed in and sat down next to me and comfortably positioned my one-year-old sister on her lap. As we drove away, I could hear the rhythm of the horse's hooves. I recall the feeling of the cool morning breeze as it brushed against my face. This had started out as a great adventure. After some time, the driver stopped at the bank of the San Juan River. From here, we had to make our way to the Los Aldamas train depot which was, unfortunately for me, on the other side of the river. The only way to get to the depot was to walk on the tracks of a railroad bridge high above the rushing waters.

Since Mother was holding my baby sister in her right arm, and our valise in her left, she instructed me to grab tightly on to her skirt. As we made our way across the railroad bridge, the open space between the ties revealed the river far below. Looking down made my stomach churn and my legs shake. I carefully calculated each step. My short legs could barely reach from one tie to the next. I was certain that my small body was the exact size to fit through the space between the ties, and should I trip or falter, I could plunge straight into the river below.

The sound of the waters below seemed to whisper, "One wrong step and I will swallow you up!" To add to my terror, my mother started shouting, "Hurry up Beatrice. We must get across before the train comes!" I tried to imagine which might be less painful, to fall in the river or get run over by a train. My heart was thumping so loud, that it sounded like the train was right behind me. I moved as fast as my little legs could carry me. While this whole scene seemed ordinary for my mother, and my baby sister was enjoying her ride in my mother's arms, it was truly my wildest adventure ever.

As you have guessed by now, I made it across safely, thank the good Lord. We caught the passenger train to Reynosa, our last stop in Mexico. From there, we took a ferry across the Rio Grande River. When we got off the ferry, we were in the city of Hidalgo, Texas, in the United States. We went directly to the Immigration Border Patrol Station. While there, they asked my mother some questions and then took me into a back room where there were several nurses waiting. They asked me to roll up my sleeve and scratched my left arm to administer a smallpox vaccination. Then they told us we could go on our way. Finally, we took a taxi to our destination in Harlingen.

The trip had taken an entire day, from sunrise to sunset. The streets of this Texas town had the most beautiful lampposts at every corner. They were made of decorative wrought iron with four round spheres at the top that glowed with light. This was so different from the streets in General Bravo where the moon was the only night light. But we were in the United States now. When we arrived at my grandparents' house, there was so much joy. Everyone was excited to see us and I felt loved. I also felt especially happy to return to the United States, the land where my life had begun.

Our visit to Texas ended all too soon. We were sad to leave but we had to return to our home in Mexico. Crossing back over the San Juan River Bridge was not as frightening since the driver of the carriage escorted us and carried our valise, and Mother held my hand. When we arrived home, the word quickly spread that I had received the smallpox vaccine[1]. The sore which at first was only a red spot on my arm had blistered, turned white, and was now filled with a pus-like substance. Smallpox had previously hit our small town and some had died. Everyone could point out the man in town who had survived. Visible on his face were the disfiguring scars from the blisters that had covered his entire body. It was not long before several of the women of the town came to plead with my mother to immunize their children from my sore. They knew my inoculation could save their children's lives. I don't know how they knew that this method would work, but it did! My mother agreed and told me that we would be doing a very good deed for the children in town. When the children came, she took a small needle, dug into my blister, and collected some of the oozing pus. She then scratched the arm of each child with some of the substance. Every child cried as his skin was pricked. Oh how much my arm ached by the time the last child had been inoculated! Mother said that because of what we did, I had provided the children with immunity against this deadly

---

1 *"The English physician, Edward Jenner, noticed that milkmaids who developed cowpox, a less serious disease, did not develop the deadly smallpox. In 1796, Jenner took the fluid from a cowpox pustule on a dairymaid's hand and inoculated an 8-year-old boy. Six weeks later, he exposed the boy to smallpox, and the boy did not develop any symptoms. Jenner coined the term "vaccine" from the word "vaca" which means, "cow" in Latin."*

disease for the rest of their lives. Soon all the vaccinated children had a scar on their arm. Mine became exceptionally large, most likely a result of all that tampering. I later realized that my mother had offered me up as the sacrificial lamb for the health of the town, and I still bear the mark to prove it. I saw how happy the parents were for their children's welfare.

At this time, I also began to realize how much love and attention my baby sister received from both my mother and stepfather. They were very happy with their new daughter. Very often I felt left out, and deep down, I wanted to know more about my own father. I had so many questions about him. Where was he? What did he look like? Did I look like him? Would I ever get to meet him? If I did, would he like me? When I saw my little sister and other girls sit on their father's lap, or kiss their fathers goodbye, I wanted so much to cry. I wanted hugs and kisses too. My heart screamed out, "Where is my father?" I knew so very little about him. My mother was very silent about anything concerning my father. I had heard that he was handsome, well educated, and very polite and proper. I was told that he was living somewhere in south Texas. So why didn't he come to see me? I kept all this longing within me. My heart wanted some answers, but these questions, for the most part, would never be answered. It was not until much later in my life that I learned that my father's relatives had wanted to see me and be part of my life. But my grandparents would have nothing to do with it. They warned my mother that if she let me visit them, they might take me away, and she would never see me again.

I started school on April 27, 1919, my fifth birthday. My teacher's name was Lolita, and she was not married. In those days, female teachers were not supposed to marry. She didn't want to accept me into her class because she thought I was too young; all the other children started at seven. Señorita Lolita changed her mind when my mother had me show her that I could say all the alphabet and count to twenty. By June, only two months later, school ended. I earned better grades than the children who had been in school all year long. I stayed at this school for three years. The school was a two-room building, one for boys and one for girls. The back yard was large, and a fence separated the boy's playground from the girl's. The toilet was an outhouse. We had no heater or fan. When it was cold I would wear the blue coat that my mother had made for me, but when it was hot we had no way of cooling off. There was no air-conditioning in those days.

At noon, the school gave us a two-hour break to eat lunch and take a nap. This was our siesta time. During this time, I preferred to do anything but sleep. So, whenever I had the chance, I would walk to Lupe Leal's house to play on the swing that hung from the tree in her backyard. I could also eat with my mother who was always there visiting and cooking something for Lupe. On the days I stayed at school, I had no lunch to eat. Therefore, I was extremely hungry when I got home. We had a large kitchen with a fireplace and a grill, but no refrigerator. In the middle, hanging from the ceiling, was a large basket that had bread, tortillas, and maybe some fruit. The food was kept high so the ants or other bugs would not get to it. Usually no one was home and there was nothing cooking. And worst of all, there was no way I could reach the hanging basket.

One day, on my way home from school, I had an idea that I was hungry enough to try. I had watched my stepfather milk the goats and I was sure I could do it. I went out and captured one of the farm goats and got under it. It started kicking so I grabbed its leg with one hand and with the other started squeezing the goat's udder. I aimed it at my mouth. As you might expect, many squirts missed and I hosed my face, hair, nose and eyes instead! Fortunately, I did get some into my mouth. I practiced every day, with less and less resistance from the goat. Sometimes when my stepfather got home and went to milk the goat he would say, "This goat is not giving much milk today." Looking back now, I think he must have suspected something, since I am sure I must have smelled like a little goat myself. I supplemented my goat's milk diet with wild berries that I found growing in the bushes around the fields. Out of necessity, I had learned to fend for myself at the age of six.

On many occasions after school, I would walk to Lupe's house, knowing I would find Mother and my baby sister there. Lupe was not in good health and Mother would cook dinner for her and her family. The mail from the city was dropped off at her neighbor's house. For that reason the man of the house was given the title of Town Postmaster, even though he didn't know how to read or write. I would go to his house to check if I had received any letters, since I was already writing to my Aunt Severita whom I missed very much. On one particular day, I stayed at the Postmaster's house for quite a while. You see, every time someone came in, the postmaster would ask me to check the pile on the counter for letters. I was a pretty good reader, even at age seven, and could sound out the words phonetically. An old man came in and told us his name. He asked the postmaster to check and see if he had received any mail that day from his children who were living in the U.S. The postmaster smiled and handed me the stack of letters. They waited as I examined the letters one by one looking for the man's name. Finally, I found one that looked like his name. As I started to pronounce it, he said, "Yes, yes, dear, that's my name. Please, won't you open it for me?" Then he said, "Oh please my dear, won't you read it to me since I don't know how to read."

I read the first two lines that said, "We hope you are doing well. We are all good here," and then I got stuck. It was, "grrraaaci..."

"Oh," said the man. "Gracias a Dios, (Thank God), that is what it says, doesn't it, dear?"

"Yes," I said, "Gracias a Dios." And I did thank God that I was able to read so I could help out the postmaster and his customers.

Whenever I received a letter from my Aunt Severita, I was happy. Having been born in my grandparents' home with my aunts and uncles, Severita, who was eleven years older than I, loved me like a little sister. Once she knew that I could read, she started writing to me about my family in Texas, and would let me know when she was planning to come for a visit. Whenever she came, I always felt so loved. She would bring me gifts like dolls or new dresses and hair ribbons, and she would spend time with me, telling me the most wonderful Bible stories. Once, she brought me a porcelain doll which was the prettiest doll I had ever owned. I treasured that doll and carried it everywhere. A neighbor asked if she could borrow it to use as baby Jesus in her Nativity scene. She called it El Niño Dios. I told her that my doll was not El Niño Dios, hugged it tightly and told her that I could not part with it. I would not give up something I treasured so dearly.

1922 - Aunt Severita at age 19

Since my grandparents, aunts and uncles had heard the gospel in Mexico, they joined the Methodist church in Donna. They had developed a deep reverence for God. Aunt Severita loved the Lord, and she overflowed with His love to me. During her visits, she would sing the most beautiful hymns about Jesus and they filled my young heart with so much love and hope and joy. I would learn the hymns and sing them over and over again after she went back to Texas.

The schools in Mexico were always closing down during times of revolutions, so there were always interruptions in my education. My aunt Severita could see that I was bright and loved school. She could also see that I was being neglected at home. On one of her visits, she asked my mother if she would allow me to go and live with them in Texas. She said grandmother wanted me to get a good education and learn English. Before Aunt Severita went back home, she asked *me* if I would like to come and live with them in Texas. I don't believe I can describe the joy I felt at that moment, but I think my heart was leaping. Without hesitation, I responded with an emphatic, "Yes!" I wanted to be with the people who made me feel cared for and so cherished. Most importantly, I wanted to know more about this wonderful Jesus whose love was pulling on **the strings of my heart**. Aunt Severita promised to return to get me the following year.

The day finally arrived, and my Aunt Severita came for me just as she had promised. How happy I was to see her. She had a new set of clothes for me to wear for my special trip. I felt such excitement about going with her and looked forward to the new adventures that lay ahead. I knew that my life in Texas would include living with my grandparents and aunts and uncles, and going to school to learn English, and attending church. There I would sing hymns and learn more about Jesus by reading the Bible. I was almost nine years old now and could read Spanish very well. The anticipation of all these things made leaving my mother, step-father, half-sister and school friends, pale in comparison.

The day I left, I gave my little sister my beautiful porcelain doll because I knew she would take good care of her. My mother asked me if I still wanted to go and I said, "Yes," and hugged her goodbye. Neither one of us shed a tear. On our way out of town, I asked my aunt to stop by the schoolhouse, so I could bid farewell to my classmates, and especially my professor. I went into the classroom and told him I was leaving. He looked down sadly for a moment and then said, "God bless you, Beatrice." I waved goodbye to all my classmates and left. I heard later from my step-cousin Cipriana, that my professor had tearfully told the class that he had just lost his best pupil.

My sister Theodora Rutoskey, age four;
and me at age eight

Chapter 3

My New Family

Train a child in the way he should go, and
when he is old he will not depart from it.

PROVERBS 22:6

My life in Texas was so very different. I now belonged to a
family where there was a mother, a father, aunts, uncles, and
cousins all around me. Our house in Donna was large and had no
heater. During the colder months, it was customary to take coals
out of the wood stove, and place them in a tub with ashes. The tub
was then carried to the center of the living room for heating, so the
women, or anyone else who wanted to, could gather round. It was a
family tradition to eat dinner and then gather. All the women in this
family had beautiful voices, so we would sit and sing hymns which I
quickly memorized. Everyone harmonized and it sounded heavenly to
me. During the summer time, we usually sat out on the front porch to
enjoy the evening breeze and some good old-fashioned conversation
about the day's events. We also shared riddles and recited poems and

occasionally, one of the older family members would tell a family story. After everyone went to bed, I usually stayed up to read my Bible and memorize verses and psalms. For many years I continued this habit of reading at night by the kerosene lamp. I also used this time for doing homework. I will always treasure the memory of those winter and summer evenings by the coals or on the porch. By participating in these gatherings, I learned about my family history.

One evening, my Uncle Librado Cantu, recalled the story of when the family first arrived in Texas. He found a job with a construction company and was taught the trade of bricklayer, earning forty cents a day. The city of Mission was building the first agriculture pump station in the Rio Grande Valley. The station would have a brick chimney over a hundred feet tall and six feet in diameter. As the chimney was nearing completion, the workers inside the building decided to fire-up the boiler, paying no attention to the fact that there were men on the outside adding the final rows of decorative bricks to the top of the chimney. My uncle was at the bottom of the chimney hoisting the bricks up to the workers, when suddenly there was a horrible accident. Because of the heat from the boiler, the two men working at the top of the chimney fell one hundred feet to their death. The bricks came down with great force, killing and injuring several men on the ground. There were a few men (maybe four or five) who were critically injured. Amongst them was my Uncle Librado. He received severe internal injuries, was in immense pain and coughing up blood. A doctor was called. He examined the injured men and said there was no hope for them. He prescribed morphine for their pain so they could die in peace. His instructions were not to feed or give them any water. My grandmother, Mama Severita, was not about to give up hope on her son and did not let the doctor administer the pain medication. Uncle Librado, in his agony, pleaded for water. Moved by her compassion she disobeyed the doctor's orders, and gave him water to drink.

The next morning the men that had been given the morphine were dead, but thanks to my grandmother's faith in God and her instincts, Uncle Librado survived. It was a miracle! When the doctor arrived he was astonished and said he would give him medication for his complete recovery. Mama Severita told the doctor that it was clear to her that it was not his medication that was healing him, but it was the Lord. Not only did he recovery completely, but he lived another sixty years.

The chimney is still standing and has been recognized as a historical landmark. The accident, however, must have never been recorded because the city's history books state that it is a "mystery" as to why the decorative row of bricks was never completed. Perhaps it was because accidents involving Mexican workers were not considered important enough to report. In addition, most of the migrant workers did not speak English which made it difficult, if not impossible, for them to defend their rights for any compensation.

When I arrived in Texas, I began attending the Spanish-speaking Methodist church. My Sunday-school teacher, Eustacia Escobar, soon found out I could easily learn long poems and psalms by heart. She gave me big parts in the Sunday-school plays at Christmas time and all other holidays. They had prizes for the child who read the most chapters of the Bible and I always read the most. Since I had already finished second grade in Mexico, I was already quite skilled in reading Spanish. Not only that, but I also had an ardent desire to read the Bible every day. I loved to participate in church activities and always looked forward to Sundays.

There were so many demands on my grandmother's life, yet she always had time for me and made me feel as if I had a special place in her heart. She made me feel wanted and valued. She sought out my God-given talents and did what she could to help me excel. My grandmother was in charge of the *Charity and Helps Commission* of the women's society in the Methodist church. Since she wanted to keep me busy with worthwhile things, she would take me with her to the women's board meetings. I learned how they organized their groups. Her responsibility in this group was to visit the sick and the needy. She recruited me as her companion. I remember visiting someone with typhoid fever and also a neighbor who had tuberculosis. Since the doctors did not know Spanish, I was extremely useful as an interpreter. At age nine, I was starting to recognize the value of being bilingual. I also developed compassion toward the sick and needy and whenever I discovered that someone in town was sick, I would tell my grandmother, so we could go and assist them. In spite of our exposure to so many different contagious diseases, the Lord kept us healthy. I believe that God was preparing me at a young age with the leadership skills that were so useful to me later in life.

As a new member of my Texas family, it was expected that I would share in the household chores. Fetching the day's milk from a distant farm was a job no one wanted. I was told that this would be my chore. It required going to the dairy farmer twice a day, once in the morning and once in the afternoon. I didn't mind going in the afternoon, it was the morning run that I found unpleasant. Since I didn't want to be late for school, I had to get up with the roosters at five o'clock in the morning and walk the mile to the dairy farm. As I look back now, I realize that this was a lot to ask of a nine-year-old girl. Although I was sometimes afraid to go alone, I remember comforting myself with a Psalm I had learned in Sunday school.

"The Angel of the Lord encamps around those that fear Him and He delivers them." As I walked along the border of the canal, I remember always leaving enough room for the angel of the Lord to walk beside me.

In order to get to the dairy farm, I had to cross the large canal which was about forty or fifty feet wide. The bridge across was a one-foot wide wooden plank. This one particular morning, I took off early with my milk bucket in hand. I walked along the canal and then crossed over the bridge. Most of the time, I arrived at the dairy farmer's house before any of his other customers. Mr. Bailey would go milk the cows and then fill my bucket. He had told me that I could help myself to his mulberry trees. So, while he milked the cows, I had a mulberry breakfast. They were so delicious; it didn't matter to me if my lips, teeth, and tongue turned purple. That could be changed with a glass of milk once I got home. I paid Mr. Bailey and started walking home. I came to the narrow bridge and, as usual, hung on tightly to the bucket trying not to spill the milk as I kept my balance. Just as I reached the middle of the canal which was about seven feet deep, my foot missed the plank, and I fell into the water.

Down, down, down I went. The milk in the bucket was replaced with water. As I sank into the canal and my feet touched the muddy bottom, I remembered what my mother had taught me. "If you ever fall into the canal," she had said, "when you hit the bottom kick yourself back up. Take a breath, and then hold your nose when you go back down." That was exactly what I did. Finally, I pushed myself over to the shallow part where my head was now above water. I still clutched the water-filled bucket and used it to wash my muddy shoes. I made it home startled, shivering and soaking wet, but I had saved the milk bucket and, more importantly, the angel of the Lord had saved me. From then on, my grandfather went to fetch the morning milk and I only had to do it in the afternoon. "All things work together for good to those who love the Lord." Romans 8:28.

My grandparents were truly compassionate people. Though they had twelve children of their own, they had also taken my cousin, Arcadio and me in as well. Arcadio was an orphan and just three months younger than I. Nine of us lived in the house: my grandmother and grandfather, five of their own children, the youngest son being Benjamin Junior. Uncle Bennie was only fourteen months older than I, and I always considered him and cousin Arcadio more like my brothers.

Papa Benjamin was working as a hired farmhand for a Jewish man at the time. One day, the farm owner was near the horses and he called my grandfather to come over to him. He told him that the farm pony could no longer stay with the family and should be killed. When my grandfather asked him why, he told him that the pony had caused the death of his eight month old son. His son had crawled out the back door where the pony had been tied. Somehow, the young child had become entangled with the rope and startled the pony. The young horse pulled away and the tangled rope choked the child. According to his Jewish beliefs, any animal that killed a person had to die. "I have to kill him, but I just can't do it," he said. Grandfather could see that the farm owner was very distressed about the situation and offered to deal with the matter for him. Grandfather brought the pony home. Immediately, our entire family fell in love with him. He was a beautiful chestnut brown quarter horse with a blaze on his forehead and white socks on all four legs. Seeing how thrilled we were, how much we loved him, and realizing his value, grandfather, like the former owner, could not find it in his heart to end the life of this little animal. We named him Pony.

1928 (L to R) Daniel Cantu, Mama Severa,
Benjamin Jr. and Papa Benjamin Cantu Sr.

My cousin Arcadio and I would take turns taking care of Pony. Soon Pony was large enough for us to ride and take into the fields to eat grass. One day, my friend Rosa was with me and she wanted to ride Pony. She climbed on his back and immediately Pony leaned forward, lowered his front legs, and slid her right off, straight into the grassy ditch. She wasn't hurt, but she didn't want to try and ride him again. Pony knew whom he wanted on his back, and it wasn't Rosa! Pony grew to be a beautiful horse and my grandfather eventually sold him for a good price.

My mother, Paula, would come to visit us once a year. During her summer visits, she usually found work and stayed for several weeks. I remember one summer when I was about ten, my mother and other family members found work in the cotton fields. They took my cousin, Arcadio and me with them, so we would not have to stay home alone.

It was early morning and we were each assigned our rows. We tied sacks around our waists and started picking the cotton. After a while, I felt pretty comfortable with the job. At one point, I reached for the next cotton ball, and noticed that something looked different. As I looked closer, I saw the head of a large rattlesnake hidden under the cotton ball. His long body was coiled on the ground. I froze for a minute, but instead of screaming, I untied my small sack and gently laid it on the ground marking the spot. Then I quietly stepped away. When I felt that I had gone far enough, I ran, like a deer, to tell my grandfather. I stuttered for what seemed like a minute while my grandfather said, "What is it, what is wrong?"

"A snake, a snake!" I finally blurted out. My grandfather ran to the wagon and grabbed the four-foot post that helped steer the horses, and took off running. I ran with him. He was so thankful that I had marked the spot with my sack. The snake was still there. My grandfather struck it over the head and pinned it to the ground with the post. Frantically, the snake lashed its body back and forth. I remember hearing the rattler make a loud noise, but Grandfather held its head firmly to the ground until it died. After he had killed it, he stretched out the snake. It was about four feet long. Everyone in the field came to see it. My cousin Arcadio, who had watched the whole thing, was very excited and begged for the rattle, so my grandfather cut it off the snake and gave it to him. Arcadio was so proud of that rattle, and took every opportunity to tell anyone who would listen, the story about the snake that could have killed Beatrice.

After the picking season and before returning to Mexico, my mother would sometimes buy new clothes for herself, my half-sister, and me. I was happy to see my mother when she came, but there was something that hindered us from spending much time together. Mother was a heavy smoker, and I could never tolerate the smoke. Most of the time, I could not be in the same room with her while she was smoking. I would ask her to stop, but she never would. Even back then I had many allergies and suffered much from congestion.

During the years that I lived in Texas, my mother became well known in her small town of General Bravo, Mexico. She was a close friend of Doña Felicitas who was the mid-wife, and as a result, Mother always knew who was expecting. Typically, when it was time for one of the women to give birth, my mother was there to assist. She became a great asset to Felicitas, watching and learning all the steps required for accomplishing a successful birth. When Felicitas passed away, my mother became the new town mid-wife. In her forty years of service to the women of General Bravo, she never lost a child or mother.

That was because, if she detected any abnormalities, she would send the women to China (which was the name of the neighboring town) where the doctor lived and had a clinic.

When I was about eleven, my Aunt Severita, who was the church pianist, started giving me lessons after Sunday-school. She taught me piano theory and how to read notes. Shortly afterwards, she married Longino Maldonado, and they moved away to a ranch out in the country. After she had left, the women's auxiliary set aside some church funds to pay for my weekly lessons from the piano teacher who came to the school. They also gave me a key to the church, so I could practice whenever I wanted. I loved the piano, and I never dreamed that such a marvelous thing could happen to me! God had opened a way for me to have a private music teacher. I was overjoyed!

After a month of lessons, the ladies sadly told me that they couldn't continue to pay for my lessons. When I told my teacher, she asked if my grandmother would be willing to do her wash in exchange for my piano lessons. My grandmother, of course, agreed, and I continued my lessons. When my teacher saw how enthusiastic I was, she decided to give me five lessons a week instead of one! I would go to the church after my class every day and practice. I would open up the hymnal and look for a song that used the same new notes I had learned that day, and then I would practice it all week long.

When Sunday morning came around, the minister would say, "Let us all stand and sing the song that Beatrice learned how to play this week." I was so happy that I could help out in this way. My grandmother always sat in the front row close to the piano and was very proud to see my progress. Soon they found a more experienced pianist to play on Sunday mornings. With only three months of lessons, I became the church's weeknight pianist. I did not take this responsibility lightly. I felt privileged to use my musical talent to help others sing praises to the Lord! Then at the age of fourteen, I was asked to teach the elementary Sunday-school class. I learned new children's hymns and earnestly studied the Bible. This was my first rendering of service unto the Lord and I was happy to do it freely. To me, it was a privilege.

Sundays at my grandparents' home were especially fun for me. Family members gathered at our house for lunch after Sunday-school. Many of my aunts and uncles would come, including my Aunt Severita and her husband. They now had two children, my cousins, Severita, and Samuel; it was always wonderful to see them. We typically had about seventeen people at the table. Since we didn't have running water, we would go to the canal and bring buckets of water for everyone to drink. The water in the canal came from the Rio Grande River. Since the water was muddy, we would let it sit until all the sediments settled at the bottom. Last year, in his final days of life, at age ninety-four, cousin Arcadio said to me jokingly, "We've had a long life Beatrice. I think it was because of all that muddy water we drank from the canal!"

When I was fifteen years old, I went with my Uncle Bennie (since I was never allowed to go far away by myself at that age) to visit my mother in General Bravo. This was the first time I had been back since I was eight years old. My mother and stepfather were now living in their new home and they were glad to see us. They took us for a short vacation to Monterrey, Mexico. I had never been there before. As I got older, I was allowed to go and visit my mother without an escort. Whenever I went, I also enjoyed visiting Uncle Librado's ranch which was a two-mile walk from my mother's house. Years later, on one such visit, my cousin, Stella (who was my Aunt Severita's daughter) had gone with me. We were enjoying our visit with Uncle Librado and his wife, Jesusita and lost track of time. It was not until I saw the bus pass the ranch that I realized we were going to miss the bus back home to Texas. I knew that the bus would make a stop at the depot/restaurant in Bravo for about a half hour. That would be our chance to board.

Since I had good horse-riding skills, I knew if I rode fast enough, I might make it back to my mother's house with just enough time to pick up our luggage, say goodbye to everyone, and gallop to the bus stop which was still another mile away. My Uncle Maclovio and his wife Adela, who lived next door to my Uncle Librado, had two horses, so I asked him if I could take the faster one. My uncle said that would be fine. We agreed that I would tie the horse up at the bus depot and he would ride out later and pick up the horse. Quickly, I saddled the horse, jumped up, put my cousin Stella behind me, and told her to hang on tight. As our horse picked up the pace, it was clear that the saddle had not been fastened securely. As we galloped downhill we both began flopping from side to side and back and forth. Stella frantically started yelling and screaming, I tried stopping the horse, but he wouldn't obey. Perhaps the screaming was confusing him. I finally slowed him down enough to jump off and make him stop. Then I tightened the saddle correctly. If anything had happened to Stella, I would never have forgiven myself. I loved her like a little sister and I felt responsible for her. I did not realize it then, but I was paying forward the love to Stella, her daughter, that my Aunt Severita had given to me. We made it just in time to catch the bus back home.

Chapter 4

Equipped For Speaking

"For I know the plans I have for you," declares the Lord, "plans to prosper you, plans to give you hope and a future."

JEREMIAH 29:11

The first thing my grandparents did when I arrived in Texas was to enroll me in public school. In that first year, I completed kindergarten and first grade. In Mexico, math had been my favorite subject. Since I had already completed the third grade in Mexico, I already knew more mathematics than was taught in Texas in the first grade. I started attending the elementary school in East Donna, which was where most of the Spanish speaking community lived. This school only went up to the third grade. In the third grade, I was elected class secretary, and my best friend, Consuelo was the class president. Consuelo and I loved school and wanted to make it fun for everyone, so we would have weekly meetings and prepare a skit. We would then select classmates and ask them to practice with us. We presented a skit every Friday.

After I had finished the third grade, I transferred to Donna Central Elementary School. Because it was far away, about half of the Hispanic children dropped out. At this school, the majority were English-speaking students. By then, I was able to communicate well in English. There was no transportation from East Donna, so I had to walk two miles. I loved school and always wanted to do my very best, so to me, it did not matter how far I had to walk. I completed fourth through eighth grades there. In this school, I had several teachers I liked very much. But there was one I did not particularly care for. Her name was Mrs. Powell. Many of the Mexican-American children felt like she did not care about us. One day during lunch, she approached me saying, "Beatrice, I see you don't participate much in class." She was referring to my eighth-grade declamation class (public speaking).

"That's because you don't like Mexicans and you only call on the white kids," I boldly stated.

"Who told you that I don't like you?" she asked.

"No one has to tell me. We all see it." I replied.

I think that was the first time anyone had ever told her that. From then on, her attitude towards me and the other Mexican-American students changed. She always called on me and even gave me preference. The kids in class started to call me the "Teachers Pet." I came to believe that Mrs. Powell genuinely loved all of us, and she became one of my favorite teachers!

Declamation was my favorite subject. I learned many poems and presented them to the class. In the eighth grade, we had a program in the large auditorium of the high school, and I was selected to recite a poem that evening. Everyone in town had been invited. For the occasion, my grandfather had personally purchased some beautiful material for me. It looked like silk. He said that since I was an excellent seamstress, I should make myself a new dress for my presentation. The material was a soft peach color. I can still remember how beautiful my dress turned out and how well it fit me. The night of the program, I recited the poem, *Being Brave at Night,* by Edgar A. Guest. It was the highlight of my declamation days. Even now at age ninety-five, I can still say the poem word for word.

After reciting my poem, the audience applauded, and I had the wonderful feeling of knowing that I had done something exceptionally well. Later on, people told me that I had made a big hit that night with my poetry recital. I had used all the gestures and vocal variety my mother had taught me when I was a child. These positive experiences helped me develop a love for both poetry and public speaking.

During my school years, Mama Severita worked doing the laundry for one of the ladies in town. This lady talked to me one day when I came by to walk home with my grandmother. She said, "Your grandmother is Cherokee Indian from Oklahoma, isn't she?"

"No, my grandmother is Mexican." I replied.

"No, she is Indian," she insisted, "I know the Cherokee Indians very well, and she is a Cherokee. I can tell by her features."

40

When I mentioned this conversation to my grandmother one day, she told me a family secret. She said, "Beatrice, I am not really Rodriguez. My grandfather's real last name was Rutledge. My grandfather was a Cherokee Indian from Oklahoma named John Baptist Rutledge."

She then told me the story of how her grandfather left his Indian village in Oklahoma when he was twelve and traveled south. He traveled over eight hundred miles and got his food by hunting with his bow and arrow. By the time he arrived in Mexico, he was a young man. Since his last name was unfamiliar to the locals and hard to pronounce in Spanish, he changed it to Rodriguez. In General Bravo, Nuevo Leon, Mexico, he met and married Angelita Quintanilla (of Spanish descent), and they had six children. I was amazed to hear this and never forgot what she told me about my Cherokee heritage.

My grandmother earned a dollar a week for doing laundry. She gave Arcadio and me each fifty cents a week for lunch, or ten cents a day. In those days, a hamburger was five cents and so was a glass of milk. One day I got tired of hamburgers. I decided to walk to downtown Donna (about 5 blocks away) where my Aunt Severita worked. There was a bakery nearby where I saw some small delicious looking pies. The baker came out, looked at me and asked, "What do you want little girl?" Even though, I was fourteen, I looked younger.

I said, "How much is the pie?"

He said, "Which one do you want?" I studied my options. There was apple, raisin, and pecan. I had never tasted a pecan pie before, but I liked the way it looked. I chose the pecan. He asked, "How much money you got?" I opened my hand and showed him my dime. He said, "You can have a pie for that dime." I went outside and ate the whole pie. It was delicious! Although it was so sweet, it didn't make me sick. That day, I decided I would walk to the bakery for lunch, as often as I could go. Every visit the baker would ask me the same question, "Which one do you want, Beatrice?" Some times I would choose the apple, and occasionally the raisin, but my favorite one was the pecan. "How much you got?" the baker always asked. The amount in my hand was always the same, and all the pies were always ten cents. At least for me they were. I never told anybody that this was all I ate for lunch. Then one day, my grandfather brought home some fresh pecans. Since I liked pecan pie so much, I planted a seed. The seed grew and became a beautiful pecan tree that still stands in the middle of Donna.

On my way to the bakery, I passed one of the stores and noticed the window display had a section reserved for the outstanding students of my school. I had written an essay on *Fire Prevention,* which had received an A+, and there it was. Over the years, my paper on penmanship and my watercolor painting of a prize-winning quilt were also displayed. I felt so honored to see my work whenever I passed by this downtown storefront window.

It was the summer of 1928. I was fourteen and in the eighth grade, and there was a recession. Jobs were scarce, especially for farmers. Of the eight in our family, no one could find a full-time job. I had heard the Dunn's Canning Factory in Donna might be hiring, so I went to apply.

While I was waiting in the office for an interview, a delivery truck arrived at the factory. The driver began to speak to the owner of the cannery, Mrs. Dunn, a Jewish widow. She saw me in the office and asked, "Do you understand what this man is saying?"

"Yes," I said. "I speak Spanish and I can interpret for you!" By then I spoke both languages fluently. I could also read and write Spanish, making me truly bilingual.

"Come here" she told me, "Tell him we will need to write down his name and license plate number. We will weigh his truck loaded, then unload the tomatoes and weigh the truck again. Then we will calculate and pay him for the actual weight of the tomatoes." I gave the driver the instructions, translating everything Mrs. Dunn had told me. With my natural gift for mathematics, I was able to calculate in my mind how much to pay the driver. The truck driver pulled out and to my surprise, there was a long line of trucks full of tomatoes waiting to be weighed. So, I stayed and helped Mrs. Dunn until the last truck drove away. Needless to say, without an interview, I was hired on the spot.

Before long, Mrs. Dunn trained me for a new position. My next job was to oversee the ladies who were peeling the scalded tomatoes. I can vividly remember the blisters on their hands. They didn't wear protective gloves back then. My job was to make sure that all the tomatoes were thoroughly peeled. It still makes me smile when I remember that at fourteen years of age, all the ladies called me Mayordoma (Manager). When someone finished a bucket they would call me over to check it. Then, I'd get one of the men to carry the buckets to the next station where they would be canned. Mrs. Dunn gave me a bag full of nickels every day. I would pay each lady a nickel per bucket, and then hand her an empty one. Dunn's Canning Factory provided jobs for women who desperately needed work to support their families. They could earn up to a dollar a day. A dollar's worth of groceries could feed a family of four for a whole week. This was such a blessing for those households where the father could not find full-time employment.

Mrs. Dunn also asked me to oversee the area where the tomatoes were put into the cans. Each can was hand packed. After filling the cans, they were placed on the conveyors where they received lids and labels. They were now ready to be packed and shipped. My job was to go from one station to another and oversee the factory workers. For the duties of a plant supervisor, I was only paid ten cents an hour. I would work twelve hours a day and get one dollar and twenty cents. I never asked for a raise, even though I believe she would have given it to me since she was very pleased with my work. I was just so glad I didn't have to blister my hands peeling tomatoes. Although my salary was modest, Mrs. Dunn would occasionally give me presents. Once she gave me a beautiful dress made of a red and white printed fabric.

One day, Mrs. Dunn took a picture of all the employees and she placed me in the middle of the group, right by her side. When she showed me the picture she said, "How nice you look standing next to me. I think it would be very nice if you would marry my son Ezzel." I politely rejected her offer. Although her son was very handsome, that did not matter to me. I didn't even care that they were very wealthy. This was my very first marriage opportunity, but it came at a time when I was not yet thinking about marriage.

I worked at the cannery for two summers while I was in school. I gave my entire paycheck to my grandparents since I was the only one who could find a steady job. These were hard times, and we were a large family. I also obtained a second job as a clerk in a variety store owned by Vicente Yanes. I worked one day a week on Saturdays from one in the afternoon to ten o'clock at night. After work, my grandfather would come and walk me home. I earned one dollar and fifty cents for the entire day and kept these earnings for my expenses.

With this money, I could buy tennis shoes for twenty-five cents or a pair of patent leather dress shoes for one dollar and fifty cents. Fabric was a nickel a yard, so I could make myself a whole dress for fifteen cents. My Aunt Severita had taught me how to sew when I was ten years old, so I would use my Sunday afternoons for this. I used this skill to make my clothes as well as for others, including my cousins, grandmother, aunts, and friends. Once, my great aunt Angelita, Mama Severita's younger sister, walked four miles from Alamo, Texas to have me make her a new dress. I finished the entire dress that afternoon and she went home delighted. She told me that she could not find anyone that could make a dress that would fit her as nicely as I could. After I got married, I also made dresses for my mother-in-law. I actually had people offer to pay me for making dresses.

People from my generation were very resourceful and recycling was commonplace. For example, people would reuse the chicken feed sacks to make clothing. At first these sacks were made of plain unbleached cotton. The only challenge was to try and remove the product logos that were printed on the sacks. Sometimes it just didn't seem worth the bother, so it was not uncommon to find words like "southern best" or other slogans on handmade clothing. Many companies saw this reuse as a marketing opportunity and started using a variety of colorful cotton fabrics as sacks for flour, sugar, beans, rice, cornmeal, grain, and salt. In 1925 the logo was printed on paper labels which could be removed.

The women who quilted selected which brand to purchase based on the fabric of the sack. I selected the fabrics for making dresses. Dreaming of someday having daughters of my own, I began sewing little girls' dresses. I would visit the department stores for ideas for my own creations. When friends or relatives gave birth to baby girls, my gift to them was always a newly sewn dress. The ribbon and lace were only one cent per yard, so I could afford to beautifully decorate the dresses. I made beautiful dresses for my Uncle Bennie's daughters: Stella, Emma, Dahlia and Irma. When I finally had my own daughters, it was my delight to make their clothes. Now, sewing is a family tradition. My daughters also enjoy sewing. Now, at age ninety-six, no one can make dresses that fit me as well as the ones my daughter Alice makes.

Times continued to worsen, and soon we found ourselves living in what was later called the Great Depression. I was brokenhearted and cried the day my family told me I had to drop out of school to get a full-time job. I loved school, and I had wanted so much to graduate from high school. But very few had the opportunity to do this. Less than one-forth of the young men at my school graduated and the number of girls who finished was even smaller. Even though I had to drop out when I was sixteen, I continued my devotion to studying the Word of God.

Chapter 5

The Comforting Spirit

You will receive power when the Holy Spirit
comes on you; and you will be my witness...
to the ends of the earth.

ACTS 1:8

When I was about sixteen, we heard that the Pentecostals or "Hallelujahs" as they were disrespectfully called, had come to Donna. Jose Guerra was one of the new converts who had come with Earl and Betsy Carter to evangelize. Hoping to spread the word, they held evening meetings in the Zuniga family's front yard so that neighbors or passersby might feel free to join in. We were curious to see what this group was all about. On one occasion, Uncle Bennie and his friend Raul Vera who were in their teens, decided that they would play a prank on the noisy worshippers, whom they considered irreverent. Our customary form of worship in the Methodist church was very quiet. These Pentecostals were very noisy. They praised God loudly and when they prayed, they spoke in tongues we could not understand. The plan was that Raul would overturn the table with the lamp while they were praying and Bennie would turn on the hose and rain water on them. The plan was not at all successful. The hose did not reach and barely sprinkled the worshippers. Not wanting to get caught, they abandoned the plot to overturn the table and the scheme failed.

As it turned out, Jose Guerra was a distant relative and he invited our family to the evangelistic meetings. Uncle Bennie was now more curious about the group and went. The next time, he invited my grandmother and me. During the meeting, someone started speaking in tongues. I picked up one of the odd sounding words, "Tekel." When I got home, I told everyone that I could speak in tongues too, so I raised my hands and jumped around and mimicked them saying, "Tekel, Tekel, Tekel." That following Sunday morning, we all went to the Methodist church. The preacher opened the Bible to the book of Daniel and read Chapter 5. His sermon was about the handwriting on the wall of King Belshazzar's palace. The fingers of a man's hand appeared and wrote the words: "Mene, Mene, Tekel, and Upharsin." That morning the minister preached on the word "Tekel" and it's meaning as interpreted by Daniel. "You have been weighed in the balances and found wanting." How exposed and what shame I felt for mocking the woman. Through that sermon and the word "Tekel," God had shown me that He weighs hearts and mine had been found lacking.

We continued attending the Methodist church but would occasionally attend the Pentecostal home meetings. About two years later, Uncle Bennie announced that he was leaving home to find work somewhere in west Texas. Before leaving town, he wanted to inform the church members of his decision, so he went to the Pentecostal meeting.

While everyone was praying, he was baptized in the Holy Spirit and spoke in tongues. He continued praying until the minister told him it was already one o'clock in the morning and everyone had gone home and he should too. Uncle Bennie said he did not want to stop praying if this joy he felt would leave him. The minister told him it would not leave. When Bennie got home, he woke everyone up and told us he had been baptized in the Spirit and was now the happiest man in the world. He would not be leaving town after all. My grandfather protested, "Those Holy Rollers don't know how to worship God. All they do is shout 'Hallelujah'!" Everyone in the house told Bennie to be quiet and go to bed!

One Sunday morning, the Methodist minister, Reverend Benito, was teaching from the book of Acts, Chapter 2. He explained that speaking in tongues was the manifestation of the Holy Spirit for the early Christians but didn't apply today. My uncle spoke up and explained how he had received the Holy Spirit by speaking in tongues, and now understood that it was also for us today. I was nineteen years old and as the church secretary, I was sitting in the front row taking the minutes. I asked for permission to speak and pointed out to Reverend Benito that Verse 39 of Chapter 2 says, "The promise is for you and your children and for all who are far off; for all whom the Lord our God will call." Reverend Benito looked at me and said, "Oh, so you want the Holy Spirit too? Well, go find it where your brother found it!" He said I need not return to the Methodist church and that I should surrender my position as the Sunday-school secretary. I was not welcome there anymore. This rejection made my heart ache.

From that point on, my grandmother, Uncle Bennie and I started attending the Pentecostal home meetings regularly. One night, they were preaching about the baptism of the Spirit. They started singing the hymn, *Jesus, Sweetest Name I Know,* and the words and music touched my heart. When they reached the part of the song that said, "All my life was wrecked by grief and strife; discord filled my heart with pain. Jesus swept across these broken strings, and now I sing again," I began to weep. I was still heartbroken that I had been kicked out of the Methodist church for speaking up in defense of my belief in the truth in God's Word. The Holy Spirit fell upon me that night. I was anointed and began to speak in other tongues and was filled with an unspeakable joy. The Spirit had come to comfort me. One night my grandmother also received great joy from the Spirit. As we were walking home from the meeting she was singing, dancing, and praising God.

Two weeks after receiving the baptism of the Holy Spirit, some believers of the Apostolic church came to speak to us regarding water baptism into the name of Jesus Christ. They pointed us to Acts 2:38 in the Bible that clearly explained it. That Sunday, five people were baptized. I asked if I could be baptized the next Sunday. I realized it would be very difficult to get permission from my grandfather, but I knew it was what I wanted.

The following Sunday, several members of the church came to pick me up. My grandfather was home that morning, and I knew he wouldn't let me go if he discovered I was going to be baptized. I asked my grandfather if he would be willing to go buy meat for dinner. He said he would be happy to, but didn't have any money. I quickly volunteered to give him as much as he needed. As soon as he left for the store I grabbed my clothes and towel and off we went to my baptism.

It was February 26, 1934, a cold winter day and the water in the canal was chilling, but my heart was burning with love for the Lord.

Four other converts and I were baptized that day. One of the sisters covered me with a big blanket after I was baptized. How joyful I was that day! Now there were two of us baptized in our house, my uncle and I. After my baptism, the members of the church began to lovingly call me "Bellita", and the name has remained to this day.

One morning, soon after my baptism, Mama Severita told me she had dreamt a very interesting dream. She said that she and I were walking down a road and had come to a river. She saw that the drawbridge was up and there was no way to cross. In the dream, we had both noticed a long chain that was used to lower the bridge. As she went to pull it, the guard said, "No not you; the young girl will bring it down." After she told me her dream, I felt that I understood what it meant spiritually. The Lord wanted to use my life to help others cross over from being separated from God, into His presence by means of the bridge, which is Jesus Christ. I told my grandmother and we both remembered a line from our favorite hymn, *I've Crossed Over Jordan to Canaan's Fair Land, and This is Like Heaven to Me.* Mama Severita kept going with us to church and soon she too was baptized in the Spirit and into the name of the Lord Jesus Christ. My cousin Arcadio and eventually, many of our family members came to the Lord and were baptized. I praise the Lord that my testimony and witness for Christ was the bridge that many used to cross over from disbelief into faith.

During the early years of my Uncle Bennie's conversion and mine, my grandfather often tried to persuade us to abandon the total commitment we had to the Lord and His gospel. He was not interested in accepting the faith or being baptized in the name of Jesus. He was especially bothered that I was going to evening church meetings and staying out until midnight. One night, Uncle Bennie and I came home late from a meeting held across town and my grandfather was still up. He said, "Beatrice, I have never laid a hand on you, but if you continue to come home late with Bennie, you will see that I know how to discipline you too. My daughters are not the type of girls that stay out late at night!"

When I heard this, I lifted up my hands and said with true joy in my heart, "Glory to God. I will be glad to suffer reproach for my faith in the Lord Jesus." My grandfather looked at me, shook his head and walked away. He knew by my response that nothing would stop me from worshiping the Lord and he never did lay a hand on me. About five years later, he told me that he had had a dream that impressed him very much. He dreamed that he was fishing and had caught two little fish which he reeled in and dropped into his bucket. He threw in the line again and this time he pulled out a gigantic human head. He was quite surprised when the head spoke to him and said, "I am the God of the fathers, Abraham, Isaac, and Jacob. And those two little fish you have captured in the bucket are Benjamin and Beatrice. You must let them go to preach the gospel of Jesus Christ." From that day on, Papa Benjamin never stopped us in our gospel work or church activities. Shortly after, and close to the time of his death, Grandfather too asked for baptism into the name of Jesus.

For lack of a formal meeting place, we met in homes which were out in the country. Many wanted to attend the meetings but we had a limited number of cars. In order to get as many as we could into one car, I would often volunteer to ride on the running board of a Model-A Ford. I would hang on with one arm through an open window. I enjoyed doing this on warm summer nights and loved to feel the wind across my face. The maximum speed of cars back then was thirty-five miles per hour and most people only drove about twenty-five, so riding on the outside was pretty safe and enjoyable. One week we had meetings for the sole purpose of praying for the sick. Canuto Garcia and his wife Inocencia, who were not Christians at that time, (but relatives of my friend Tomasita) wanted to attend since they had heard the testimony of many in town who had been healed and because Inocencia had been very ill. They and other members of their family were driving from Garciasville to Mission. They stopped to see Tomasita to get directions to the meeting place. Instead, she gave them directions to my house in Donna and told them to ask me if I would accompany them as their guide. They came to my house and introduced themselves and asked if I would do them this favor. I agreed and since I could not go anywhere alone, I took my eight-year-old cousin, Daniel. The car was already filled to capacity, so my cousin and I had to sit in the back on someone's lap.

We traveled for a while, and I was enjoying the conversation, when suddenly I realized we had missed the turn. I told the driver, Canuto who quickly put on his brakes, started backing up, but suddenly hit the brake again when he felt the right back end of the car drop. I looked out the window and saw that the rear right wheel had gone off the road and was hanging in mid-air over the ditch. The front right wheel was barely gripping the road. Canuto froze not knowing what to do and all the women in the car started crying. I am not sure where my courage came from, but I knew someone had to take action. This Model-A had only two doors in the front, and the back seat only had small windows. Since I was very thin, I decided to squeeze out the window and jump into the ditch. I then pulled my cousin through the window as well, moved him away from the car and helped him climb back onto the road. I thought that if the weight was lighter on the right rear side, we might have better traction on the left side where the tires were firmly on the road. I also got back on the road and told Canuto to put the car in forward drive and step on the gas while I pushed the car from the outside until we got the tires back on the road. I believed that with the Lord's help we would succeed, and we did. I felt compelled to stand against any counter force that was trying to keep us from getting to that healing prayer meeting that night. When we arrived at the gathering, every one of us was already thanking and praising God. We prayed for Inocencia's healing and the entire family received the gospel and accepted Christ as their Savior. Some years later, Canuto Garcia became a pastor and later became bishop for South Texas. Inocencia had two more children and lived to be ninety-three years old.

Another time (several years later), we were traveling from Mission to Edinburg to go to a home church meeting. My friend, Zoila Reina and I were sitting in the rumble seat in a Model-T Ford. Guadalupe Garcia (who later became my brother-in-law) and his wife, Petra were in the front seat. To accommodate the many who wanted to go to the meeting, he had attached a trailer to the car. On the trailer were two benches which could seat about four passengers each. After being on the road for a while, I noticed that the hitch was coming loose and my first instinct was to try to grab it. Before I could do it and probably a good thing for me, the hitch pulled away.

We watched as the trailer with eight people sitting on the benches, rolled away and then veered to the left and off the road, straight into the shallow ditch. I watched as the trailer finally stopped and dumped both benches and passengers onto the grass. We stopped the car and ran down into the ditch to see if everyone was OK. While everyone was a little shocked, no one had been injured and even the benches were intact. The driver of a passing car that had seen us in the ditch notified the police in the next town of the accident. The police and ambulance showed up to check on the situation. When I saw them, I ran up and told them that everyone was fine. After the police had gone, we hitched the trailer securely back on to the car. With everyone back on the benches, we drove off to Brother Canuto Garcia's home to rejoice and praise the Lord.

Around 1934, wanting to see how the Apostolic Assembly was organized in Monterrey, Mexico, my Uncle Bennie, Canuto Garcia, Adela and Tomasita Saenz and I, decided to visit the church there. At that time, Canuto was the only one with a car, so we went in his. We stopped in Laredo, Mexico where we enjoyed the hospitality of church members. While there, we learned to our surprise, that all religious services were forbidden and the Christians of Mexico could no longer worship in public. The former President, Plutarco Elias Calles (1924 – 1928), a proclaimed atheist, had written a law against religious freedom. It was mainly against the Catholic Church but endangered all Christians. People believed that the main reason for the persecution was that he opposed the heavy hand by the Vatican that required the Mexican Catholic Church send the offerings of the Mexican people to Rome. While Rome prospered, Mexico suffered economic depression. President Calles wanted this money to remain in Mexico.

The Mexican soldiers killed thousands of priests and anyone suspected of aiding them. The Catholics rose up in opposition to the anti-clerical laws and declared war. This warring period was known as the Cristero War. After his term in office, Calles appointed himself Jefe Maximo (Head General, 1928 – 1938), which allowed him the political power to continue suppressing the church. Because of this, all religious worship had to be done in secret. After learning this, we left Laredo and continued on to Monterrey.

We visited with the pastor and he verified that the Christians in Mexico were still under a period of persecution. They told us that in spite of this religious turmoil, many were still becoming Christians. During our visit, some new converts wanted to be baptized. We discussed how we could do this without endangering their lives, as well as our own. The pastor knew of a place hidden in Las Mitras in the Sierra Madre mountain range, just outside the city. We went with them by train to the small town of La Huasteca. When we got off, a group of people recognized us as Christians and tauntingly began barking at us. I asked why they were doing this and a lady I was with said it was because they considered all Christians to be dogs. Having reached the mountains, we walked through the woods until we came to a place where there were three beautiful crystal clear streams. It was here that the new converts were baptized.

During our stay, we were invited to take a tour of El Obispado, a monastery that was located at the top of a hill in Monterrey which had been shut down. Our tour guide told us that there was a secret underground tunnel from El Obispado to the statue of the Virgin of Guadalupe located at the bottom of the hill. The priests used the tunnel during the height of the persecution to hide. Our visit in Monterrey was just over a week. We returned home praising God for His protection and were now even more thankful for the religious freedom we had in America!

Whenever possible, I would go and visit my mother in Mexico. On one of these visits, I went to see my uncle Maclovio and Aunt Adela. I always talked about the Lord and prayed with them. While there, Senorita Raquel, the local town schoolteacher, came by to say hello. After chatting for a while, Raquel, my two cousins, Ercilia and Eluteria, and I, decided we would walk to the nearby hill to search for fossilized seashells. Because it was a very hot day, we borrowed umbrellas to shade us from the scorching sun. When leaving, my uncle said, "When you get to the top of the hill you will be closer to God; ask Him to send us rain. We have not had rain for almost a year and our corn crops are dry, and the soil is parched."

We arrived, and when I reached the summit, I remembered my uncle's request and asked the Lord with all my heart to send the rain. After a while, we noticed that it was getting dark, and we decided to head back home. Looking up we saw the clouds and felt the raindrops. How happy we were that we had borrowed the umbrellas as we ran home in the pouring rain.

The news spread on how God had answered my prayer and whenever there was a drought in Mexico, my family would send word and ask me to pray for rain. God is merciful and answers our prayers.

I always prayed for the salvation of my friends. I wanted them to hear the gospel and love the Lord. I would invite my special friend, Hortencia, to our Sunday evening services which were held on the patio of a church member's home. We had no electricity so our only light came from a kerosene lamp that hung on a nearby tree. That night, I sang a song that said, "I now have a dwelling with Christ in His glory, a garment that is white as snow. I'm hoping and praying for you to come also, for you I am praying, I'm praying for you." I felt that my words were for Hortencia.

The next day, I went to Hortencia's house to help her with her piano lesson. She was learning to play *La Golondrina*, the swallow's farewell song. Her mother came out from the kitchen saying, "I told you not to play that sad song because it gives me goose bumps!"

Hortencia asked, "Are you afraid I'm going to die? Well, if I die, you give my piano to Beatrice."

I said, "Let's play a hymn from my music book instead." So we played the song, *This Is like Heaven to Me*. After her lesson, I told Hortencia I had to go home. She said she wanted to walk me home. On the way, she said to me, "The song you sang at the church meeting last night, 'For You I Am Praying', really touched my heart. I want to be saved like you and be baptized, but my mother won't let me. She is planning a big Quinceañera party for my 15th birthday. As soon as it's over I want to be baptized."

We said goodbye and I went home, and she did too. When Hortencia got home, she ate some watermelon and began playing and spinning in circles with her little cousin. Then she started throwing up. Her mother told her to clean up the mess. She thought that she had thrown up the watermelon, but instead she was vomiting blood. Then she collapsed. At that moment, Hortencia's brother, Raul Vera, and my Uncle Bennie arrived at the house. They prayed for her and called the doctor. By the time the doctor arrived she was already dead. My Uncle Bennie came home, told me what happened and suggested I go to comfort her mother. I could not believe the suddenness of Hortencia's death. A few months later, Hortencia's mother told me to come and take the piano her daughter had wanted me to have. Since the church in Mission did not have a piano, I donated Hortencia's to them. I played that piano in church every week and never forgot my dear friend and how early her life had ended. Although Hortencia never had the chance to be baptized, I know with certainty that she had already believed and surrendered her heart to Jesus.

I had another dear friend named Senona. She was the daughter of a black family that attended our church services. They had all been baptized. On one occasion, Senona and I were going somewhere together and decided to take the bus. As soon as she boarded, she motioned that she was going to sit in the back. For the first time, I noticed the sign at the back that said, "Colored." Something in my being became agitated as I felt the anger and pain of discrimination. I told her not to go to the back of the bus, but to sit in the front next to me. I spoke these words loudly enough for the bus driver who was watching us in the mirror to hear. He must have seen the determination in my eyes because he just continued driving. Senona sat next to me until we reached our destination. Not a person spoke out against us. My daughters jokingly said that perhaps Rosa Parks might have been a descendent of my friend Senona.

Chapter 6

Peace in the Storm

Delight yourself in the Lord and he will give
you the desires of your heart.

PSALM 37:4

O n Monday, September 5, 1933, I was watching the sun set
when I noticed that Papa Benjamin and the other men of the
family were frantically digging in the yard. I wondered what they
were doing. Papa Benjamin called me over and pointing up at the
sky, said, "Beatrice, look! I have never seen clouds like this in the
sky before. This is a very bad sign. There is going to be a hurricane."
Dark gray clouds coming from the east and large gray and black
clouds coming from the west were rolling around the sky at high
speeds in all directions. The air felt different as the wind began to
blow. Papa Benjamin went inside and told the women that we needed
to prepare for a storm. By this time, the five men of the family had
secured all four corners of the roof with strong ropes. They had
secured one corner to a strong tree and placed poles deep into holes

they had dug to secure the other three corners. He then went to the store and bought plenty of food, while we waited inside and prepared jugs with drinking water.

At 9 P.M., the hurricane bore down on Brownsville, Texas, with winds of 120 miles per hour. The winds began to slow down slightly as the hurricane moved west towards our fragile home in Donna. I was sleeping when my Aunt Chalita (Gonzala) came into the bedroom screaming, "Sweetie, wake up, wake up, the world is coming to an end! Listen to the howling wind. The roof tiles are flying everywhere. Our roof is leaking, and the rain is coming in. Look out the window at that house down the road, it's on fire." When she finally stopped screaming, I heard the roaring sounds of the hurricane's fury. I realized that my mother was right when she had said I could sleep through anything, including a hurricane.

By the time I got up, it was decided that everyone would evacuate and go next door to my Uncle Victor's. He had a newer house which everyone hoped might better withstand the storm. The shortest evacuation path was from one of our windows, so the five men positioned themselves between the houses forming a human chain to help guide the women across. Since I was the youngest and strongest, I helped each one of the four women climb out the window. Then, I grabbed a set of clothes and wrapped them in a towel. I was the last one out. In blinding rain and punishing wind, I crossed the human chain. Holding on tightly from one relative to the next, I crossed from our house to the back door of Uncle Victor's house. We all made it across safely. Once inside we took off our drenched clothes and got into our dry ones. Then we all gathered together in the living room and prayed and sang all night long as the hurricane raged outside. One of the hymns very fittingly said, *Christ is our refuge in the storm.*

It was noon the next day before the wind and rain subsided. After the storm, we eventually learned that all our family members in neighboring farms and towns were also safe. The devastation had been great. The newspaper reported that skies had dumped fifteen inches of rain in the wake of the hurricane. Two feet of water and mud covered the town. Miles of citrus groves lay waste. Big yellow grapefruit and oranges floated in pools of muddy water in the torn groves. Buildings had been leveled, and hundreds were homeless. The total economic loss to the Valley was a staggering seventeen million, ten million in citrus alone. Long strings of freight cars on the Southern Pacific tracks between Mission and Harlingen were bowled over in the hurricane's fierce assault. The roofs of virtually all the smaller buildings in Harlingen had been whipped loose. The house across the street from ours turned upside down; ours had remained right side up but the one tree we had used as an anchor was uprooted. The house down the road had burned because of the electrical wires that had fallen on it. This hurricane dealt the Lower Rio Grande Valley the worst beating it had suffered in many years. To add to the tragedy, many people were now out of jobs because the citrus crop and packing plants had been destroyed.

In spite of all the devastation that year, I felt so blessed to find work doing something that I loved. My friend Tomasita had started a private Christian school for first graders in her home in Mission. Her mother, Adelita, had a large property with several buildings on it. She donated one of them to be used for church meetings. The building she lived in had a large attached structure that had been divided into two rooms which were used as classrooms. Tomasita asked me if I would be interested in teaching a second grade class. I gladly accepted the offer and moved from my grandparent's home in Donna to live with Tomasita and her mother in Mission. The cost to attend the private school was fifteen cents a week for second graders and ten cents for the first graders. Altogether, we had about fifty-five pupils. Our school day always started with prayer and a children's hymn. It was a blessing to teach, not only reading, writing and arithmetic, but also the Word of God. We regularly invited the parents to come to church services. Some parents received the Gospel and were baptized. The church grew in numbers and we had much joy in the Spirit.

My Uncle Bennie had been preaching for several years and was now the pastor in Mission. Since I had moved there to teach, I was also available to help him with the ministry. He asked me to help organize the women's society. I helped organize different work groups and we planned and held fundraisers, like making tamales and selling them for ten cents a dozen. We also collected ten cents a month from each member to start our own fund. Having felt a calling to teach, I also instructed the women of the church in the Word of God. Since many of the women could not read but had good memories, I would read them the psalms and help them memorize the scriptures.

I knew that some of my biological father's relatives lived in Mission and thought of getting in touch with them. I had so many questions to ask about my father. My only memento of him was a very old picture my mother had given me and I cherished it. Since Mission was a small town, my father's relatives soon heard that I was the new teacher at the private school. One day, by chance, I met one of my father's cousins, Victor Gutierrez, a handsome blue-eyed gentleman who worked delivering water. When he saw me walking down the street from the private school, he stopped, got out of his wagon, and came over to ask me if I was the daughter of Graciano Gutierrez. He told me that my father's cousin, Francisca, lived only three blocks down the street. I knew then that getting the chance to meet her had been pre-ordained.

The next day, I went to visit and introduced myself. She told me that my father was living in Corpus Christi and I asked if she could let me know whenever he came to town. Francisca contacted my father and informed him that I was living in Mission and wanted to meet him. The days I waited to hear from him seemed like an eternity. Finally, I received the good news. My father and his only sister Sanjuana were coming to Mission in two weeks. I prayed and thanked God. How long I had waited for this day to come! What would I say? How would I feel when I saw him?

It was March of 1934, just one month shy of my twentieth birthday. We finished teaching school that day and with anticipation and fast pace I walked over to Francisca's house. Too numerous to count were the times I had dreamed of this day. I could feel my rapid heartbeat and was aware of the excitement in my being. When I came to the door, I saw unfamiliar faces; these were relatives that I had never met before. As I entered the house, my eyes locked on someone I thought to be the most handsome man I had ever seen, and **the strings of my heart** reached out to him. The minute he stood up and walked across the room with his arms outstretched, I knew that this was indeed my father! With tenderness, he hugged me and said, "I am so happy to meet you my beautiful daughter!" I felt his body tremble as his tears began to stream down his cheeks and on to my face. Unable to utter another word, he pulled himself away and went into the kitchen; there he sat at a table and with his hands covering his face, he wept loudly. I followed him and put my arms around his shoulders and said, "All my life I have waiting for this moment. This is a great and happy day for me." I looked around and realized that everyone in the living room was weeping but from my eyes, there fell no tears. There was only the joy that comes from a long awaited desire finally fulfilled.

That day, I knew what it felt like to be in the presence of my father and to feel his embrace. In those few moments in his arms, all the years of doubts regarding his love for me vanished and I understood that he did love me and I loved him back. After our hearts were comforted, we sat and talked and had some tea. One by one, I met the others in the room, including my stunning blue-eyed, black-haired Aunt Sanjuana. I was so grateful to finally meet my father and my other relatives. Far too soon, it was time to say goodbye, but I left hoping to see my father again soon and he promised we would. The next day my father and aunt returned to Corpus Christi.

In meeting my father, I had found the missing piece in my life. It had been like salve to my wounded heart. And to know that he had found me beautiful was unbelievable. This was the very first time in my life that I had been called beautiful and the words had come from the man I had so much longed to be loved by, my father.

As fate would have it, this reunion was the only time I would ever have with my father. Three months later, he was killed in a motorcycle accident on his way to work by a thirteen-year-old boy who was driving his mother's brand new Cadillac. One precious day, one tender hug, one short exchange of loving words would be all I could hang on to. His words "My beautiful daughter," are still etched in my heart.

My father Graciano G. Gutierrez – 1911

On the day my father was killed, the news was sent to his sister Sanjuana who was in the hospital after having her appendix removed. I was told that she never left the hospital but died shortly after receiving the news. My father's brothers had also sent a telegram to Victor in Mission. Victor went to Francisca's house (the house where I had met my father) and told her he had some bad news. As he read the message, Victor collapsed and died. Francisca notified me of the tragedies but the savage death grip was not over yet. Francisca sent word to her mother, my Aunt Michaela (who was the mid-wife that had delivered me) and while everyone was attending the funerals, we received word that Michaela had died in Mexico. In my young life, my dear father and three family members whom I had met were taken away so quickly. The opportunity to build family ties with these family members was cut short and unfortunately, the deaths were all tied to the death of my father.

I felt a great loss after my father's death. Although I had church friends, I felt lonely and I missed my family. I wanted my family to come and enjoy the fellowship with us. I had heard that my grandmother's sister, Ramona owned a house and a large lot in Mission. When Ramona's husband died, she abandoned her house and moved to Alamo, Texas. I decided to talk to her about her vacant house, since I wanted to move my grandparents, my Aunt Chalita, Aunt Antonia, and my cousin Arcadio to Mission and have them live with me. Aunt Ramona said that I should go to city hall and check the status of the house. I found out that the house was about to be sold for back taxes. Since I had a job, I made an agreement with the city to make the monthly tax payments. I took possession of the house and the attached lot, and we all moved in. I was so happy that we all were back together again and that I was able to give back something to bless them, as they had blessed me.

On December 5, 1935, my Uncle Bennie and Tomasita got married. In April of 1937, the church board members asked them to move to El Paso to pastor the church there. Uncle Bennie asked me if I wanted to go with them, and I agreed. I packed up my things, said goodbye to my grandparents, family and friends. We closed down the Christian private school and I went willingly to help spread the gospel. Guadalupe Garcia became the pastor of the church in Mission. He and his wife, Petra moved into the building where we had conducted our classes. We went with no jobs and no housing, fully trusting that God would provide for all our needs, which He did. After living in El Paso for about eight months, we heard there was going to be a church convention in California and Uncle Bennie and I went. Tomasita stayed home because she was expecting their first child. At the convention, I made new and life long friends.

After the convention in California, I got a ride back to El Paso with my Uncle Bennie. When we got home, I had received a telegram informing me that I needed to be in Corpus Christi within a few weeks to attend a court hearing and settlement regarding my father's accidental death or the case would be closed. The deadline for appearing in court was near. I needed to get from El Paso to Mission and then to Corpus Christi in a hurry. I wrote my grandparents that I would be coming to Mission and that I had a ride with some friends as far as Laredo. From there I would need to take a bus. I had just enough money to get me from Laredo to Mission. When the bus arrived at the Mission bus depot, it was very late at night and pouring rain. I was only twenty-three years old, all alone and afraid to walk home by myself. I told the bus driver I lived about a mile away and would have to walk home in the rain. He told me to wait a minute while he went into the terminal office. When he came out, he said, "Get back in the bus, I'll drive you home!"

When I explained that I had no money to pay him, he said, "That's okay, you don't need to." The rain made it very difficult to see the street names, but I managed to direct him toward my house. He drove that large bus with only one passenger in it, me. My grandfather heard the noise on the street and could not believe that the Greyhound bus had brought me straight to our doorstep! Now I could prepare for my trip to Corpus Christi for the court hearing.

Unbeknownst to me, my father's brothers had entered a claim against the company that insured the Cadillac driven by the boy that had killed my father. The insurance company's attorney had asked if my father had a living heir. If so, those people, in this case me, would have to appear at the hearing. I appeared on the day of the court hearing and under oath, the attorney asked me how much my father had given me for my support. I informed him that my father had never given me any financial support. He said that my uncles had told him that he had. "But it's not so." I protested. Just then I saw my uncle pound the table in disgust.

"But he was supposed to," the attorney told me. "If you do not say this, then there is no settlement and you will lose twenty thousand dollars." he whispered to me. Even then, I was very firm. How could I lie, having laid my hand on the Bible with a promise to tell the truth? Finally, the case was over, and we had lost. I felt the pain of never having received anything from my father, not even at his death, but it was a familiar pain and one with which I had already made peace. But in my heart, one thing was very clear; I had won, not in cash, but in conscience. The court ordered that I receive the sum of $500. I gave my uncles half of that amount as a contribution towards what they had paid for my father's funeral. The remainder I deposited into a savings account.

PART TWO

He knew exactly how to tune that string
so that it made sweet music.

Chapter 7

Courtship and Married Life

My beloved is mine and I am his.

SONGS OF SOLOMON 2:16

Patricio Garcia was a Christian man who was born and raised in Donna, Texas. He was an acquaintance from my early school days. He was the seventh child of Victoriano Garcia and Maria de la Luz Moreno, born on March 17, 1917. Patricio started school in East Donna at age seven and that was where Patricio and I first met. One day, Pat was playing with the water faucet on the playground and squirted me and my friends as we passed by. Then he ran away. As he ran, I shouted, "You dummy Patricio. You got us all wet." I guess he made an impression on me that day, but it wasn't favorable. Pat and I continued in school together until 1929 when the Great Depression forced us to drop out and seek work. Patricio told me that one day when he was about fifteen, he saw me in town walking toward him and he thought, "When I grow up I would like Beatrice for my wife." Years later his wish came true.

Patricio was baptized into the name of Jesus Christ in July of 1936, in the city of Weslaco, by his eldest brother Guadalupe Garcia (who was also called Lupito). Pat was gifted with an excellent ear for music. After his conversion, he dedicated himself to the music ministry, playing the trumpet, guitar, and piano. Every Sunday Pat came to the church services in Mission, even though he lived in Donna. Pat would come to help his brother, Guadalupe who was the music pastor. Since Pat did not own a car, he would hitchhike from Donna to Mission every Sunday. Pat played the guitar while I played the piano at each service, so naturally, we became friends.

One Saturday, I had gone to the church to replace a broken string on the piano. Pat, who was visiting his brother, surprised me by walking into the church and asking me what I was doing. After I told him, he volunteered to help. I had already placed the string from one end to the other and now it needed someone to tighten and tune it. This is not an easy task as it requires someone with a good tuning ear. Pat knew exactly how to tune the string so that it made sweet music. This time my impression of Pat was favorable. It turned out that Pat had prepared a letter for me and was hoping to give it to me that morning. He asked me if I would receive it from him. I told him I would. As I took it, I noticed a tear was rolling down his face. He could not say another word, so he excused himself and left the building.

On my walk home, I opened the letter. It was a love letter in which he asked if I would accept him as my boyfriend and future fiancée. This was not a surprise to me because he had already told my cousin Arcadio that he was in love with me but that he did not know how to tell me. He had told Arcadio that he was afraid I would reject him like the others who had wanted to court me. I was not in a hurry to respond. Several weeks later as Pat was tuning the guitar to play for the Sunday service, he asked me if it was in the key of "Si." I knew he was really asking if my answer was "Yes?" I answered that it was not "Si" (Yes) but in "Mi" (me). In other words, *I* would decide when I was going to say "Yes" and *I* was not ready yet.

I was very happy with my single life and I was so in love with the Lord Jesus that I felt complete joy and contentment. Although there had been other young men at church interested in me, I did not desire another love besides the Lord's and I didn't think about marriage. I believe now that my mother's failed marriage to my father had left a wound in my heart. I had privately told the Lord that I would rather die than have a broken marriage. Why would I ever want to marry and have children who might face a life without a father? At that time, a relationship leading to marriage was just not something I wanted to consider.

That summer, I went to visit my mother in Mexico. While I was there, she asked me if I was ever going to think about getting married, so I decided to tell her about Pat's letter. I told her I was thinking a little about it, but not that much. During this visit, I saw my half-sister Theodora. She was married and had two sons, Horacio and Cesar. That day, my sister and some of her friends decided to go down to the river to bathe and invited me along. They were all very good swimmers and I was not. The river was shallow near the bank but further out it was deep and the current was very strong.

In the middle of the river was a rock island about ten feet square. All the girls, except me, swam to the island. My sister called for me to come. I said, "No, I don't swim well and I might drown." Their reply was that I shouldn't be a coward and that if they had to, they would save me. So I threw myself into the water and tried to swim across. The current quickly pulled me down. I felt my body suck in all the water. Everything turned bright yellow and that was the last thing I remember. When I woke up, I was lying on the river's edge in the middle of the puddle of water which I had coughed up. My sister, who was six months pregnant at the time, had jumped in to save my life. Once again, thanks to God and to my sister, I was spared from drowning. I returned to Texas a few days later, happy to be alive and see my family and Pat again.

Pat waited two months for my answer. He knew what he wanted and he was willing to wait. During that time, I realized that, for the first time, I felt a special affection and attraction for him. Pat was such a gentleman. He had written me a love letter and was very patiently waiting for me to reply, just like Christ wrote his love letter to us in the Bible and waits patiently for us to accept Him of our own free will. He never rushed me to make a decision. As time passed, I found myself falling deeply in love with him. However, there was still one thing that worried me and that was his age. He was twenty-one and I was going on twenty-four. I thought he was too young for me. Or, maybe I was worried because both of my mother's husbands had been much older - as was the custom then. I finally wrote him a letter and told him the problem. Pat replied quickly, saying that our age difference meant nothing to him. In my next letter, I told him about a husband I knew who always referred to his older wife as his "old woman." I told him that because of our age difference, I would have to reject his proposal. In his next letter, Pat promised me that if the Lord granted him his desire, he would never say a word about my age. I decided then that the answer in "Me" was "Si." The next time we saw each other he gave me his picture and asked for one of me.

That week I wrote and said I had a picture but I did not want to send it by mail because I had something else I wanted to give him. The next time we saw each other, to my surprise, he asked me for a kiss. He thought that the "something else" I referred to in my letter, was a kiss. What I had planned to give him was a wallet to hold my picture! I got so offended that I wanted to break up with him. I believed that it was only right to kiss someone after you were married. I felt he didn't respect me. He apologized and asked my forgiveness. We both agreed that we would wait for the day of our wedding. Then I gave him the wallet with my picture inside.

One day, Pat came by our house with cousin Arcadio. My grandfather noticed him although no one introduced him, and he asked me later, "Who is that handsome young man that came by today?" I told him that he was my boyfriend. I was happy that my grandfather approved of him. Pat asked me to marry him immediately after I had answered yes. My grandfather, however, fell very sick at that time and I told Pat that we should wait until my grandfather recovered. Unfortunately, my grandfather's health got worse and shortly after he passed away. Another year went by. Pat said that we had waited long enough and it was time to set the wedding date. Once I agreed, Pat sent word to my mother in Mexico asking her for permission to marry me. My mother did not respond for three months. Finally, one of my relatives went to visit my mother and asked why she had not answered the letter.

She was puzzled and said, "Why are they asking for my permission? Beatrice is old enough to make up her own mind. If that is what she wants and he is of her faith, then they should get married. Just tell me when to come to the wedding." Two years had gone by so, by the time I married Pat, he had grown up to be twenty-three.

Finally, the date was set for May 12, 1940. Our wedding ceremony was beautiful. Marcos (Pat's brother) played the piano and sang 'Dios Bendiga Las Almas Unidas' (God Bless These Two Hearts as One). My Maid of Honor was Margarita De Leon and her husband, Eliezer De Leon was our best man. They donated the wedding cake. Tables were set up in the church's yard and decorated. After our ceremony, we enjoyed our reception dinner. Mother came with a very special gift of freshly butchered and deliciously prepared Cabrito (a Mexican delicacy of young goat's meat). Pat's older sister, Delfina, who was an excellent cook, brought chicken that had been freshly prepared.

Right after we were married, Pat took both my hands in his and told me that he was longing to touch my left hand since every Sunday when we greeted each other at church he had only touched my right one. That day, Pat and I kissed for the first time!

The next day, we left for General Bravo, Mexico. My mother had arranged for a second wedding ceremony at her home. My Maid of Honor was Chata Guajardo and she took care of the wedding arrangements and reception. After our honeymoon in Mexico, we returned to Mission and moved into one of the buildings on the property belonging to Adela Saenz. It was the building that we had used for the Christian private school classes when we were teaching. The school was no longer in operation and Adela rented it to us as our first apartment. My Uncle Bennie and Tomasita had come back from El Paso and were again pastors in Mission and living in one of the buildings on the property.

Our Wedding Day May 12, 1940

I had prayed for my mother's conversion for seven years. One day, very soon after I got married, my prayer was answered and my mother received the Lord in her heart and asked to be baptized. She had truly repented and to my amazement, she stopped smoking on that day and never took it up again. Little by little, my mother's life went through a transformation. It was wonderful to witness the change that can happen in the life of a surrendered heart.

One day while Pat and I were going for a walk, we saw a big old abandoned house for sale. Pat and I decided that if we could buy the house and tear it down, we could reuse the wood to build our first home. We spoke to the owner and he said that he would sell it to us for twenty-five dollars. He didn't have to tell us twice; we agreed to buy it. Pat's brother, Marcos, who was a carpenter by trade, along with other unemployed church members, volunteered to help Pat dismantle the old house and clean the wood. The workers were more than happy to work in exchange for the lunchtime meal that we provided. Once the wood was ready, Marcos helped us build our house in Mission on the property next to the house that I had recovered by paying the back taxes. We used up the two hundred dollars I had saved from my dad's accidental death settlement to complete the house. Now we had a house of our own and it was all paid for. Pat and I put up panels of wood in the interior of the house. I would measure and mark the wood and he would cut and nail. Pat built a wooden chest for storing my wedding presents and I made cushions for it so it also served as a sitting area in the dining room. Pat also built a pull-down ironing board into the wall hidden by a door that closed and latched. The closet in the bedroom also served as our bathing room. We would put a tub in that room and fill it up with water from a pail. He also made shelves and cabinets in the kitchen. We put up some beautiful wallpaper in our bedroom.

When it was finally finished, we moved in and made our home ready for our first son. Ruben Edward was born at home in Mission on February 13, 1941. Dr. Walker came to the house to deliver him. Mother came from Mexico to assist me with my firstborn son and stayed for six weeks.

The summer after Ruben Edward was born, we went to visit my mother in Mexico. During our visit we would often see other members of the family. On many occasions, I saw my cousin, Ernest Cantu. Ernest was seven years younger than I. He was fortunate enough to have finished college, and was now a professor. During these years, atheism had infiltrated the public schools in Mexico and my cousin had adopted the philosophy. He told me that the first thing he would say to his students every morning was, "There is no God."

"There never has been and there never will be." they would reply in unison.

When my cousin told me this, my heart was troubled because of his unbelief, so I showed him a scripture verse in the Bible that says, "The fool has said in his heart, there is no God." Because I loved Ernest and he respected me, he knew that I was speaking to him sincerely. He knew that I was praying for him to believe in God and experience the same joy I had found. When I would visit, someone in the family would always ask me to sing a hymn, which I was always willing to do. Years later, Ernest told me that those hymns had touched him and eventually God's love found its way to his heart. He was converted and became a tremendous blessing to many as he committed his talent and training to the Lord's service. Ernest married a beautiful sister in the Lord named Ruth who is to this day, still my very dear friend. She assisted him in the work of the Lord during the time that Ernest served as a pastor in Corona and Arlington, California. He was a teacher of God's Word and for many years held the office of Director of Christian Education in the Apostolic church.

This particular visit to Mexico included an unforgettable experience. One day I was hanging the baby's diapers on the clothesline in the backyard. Since I was looking up, I did not notice the small but venomous and deadly coral snake at my feet. Suddenly, the family dog came running and jumped between my leg and the snake. The snake which had intended to strike my leg bit the dog in the mouth instead. The dog let out a painful yelp and as I looked down, I saw the snake. My stepfather, having witnessed all of this from the porch, was already running toward us with a stick which he used to kill the snake. Then he quickly took the dog, and pulling out a pocketknife, skillfully slit open the wound to extract the poison. The dog's head swelled up, but every day for about a week my stepfather nursed the wound and the dog recovered. Through the instinct and loyalty of a family dog, the Lord had protected me once again.

World War II started just eight months after Pat and I were married. All the men were being drafted to serve in the military. In 1941, Pat had to go to register for the draft. He was excused because at that time, they would not take newly married men. He had to register again in 1942, and this time he was excused because he had a dependent child. The following year, Pat was doing some farming work. That year they were excusing all the farmers from military duty. Finally, in 1944 when the war was at its peak and very few were being excused, he was summoned again. Pat and I and the church family prayed and fasted. Even our three-year-old son, Ruben, said he was praying and fasting too so that his daddy did not have to go to war. At the appointed day, Pat went to the recruiting office. As was customary, they gave him a physical examination. After his examination, the doctor told Pat he had a small hernia and because of this he would not be selected for service. We rejoiced! That same year we were blessed with the birth of our second son, Ramiro Israel. My mother came from Mexico in time to deliver him. Ramiro was born at home on November 8, 1944.

Chapter 8

Proved By Fire

So that the proving of your faith, much more precious than of gold, which perishes though it is proved by fire, may be found unto praise and glory and honor at the revelation of Jesus Christ.

PETER 1:17

It was November 11, 1946, our eldest son, Ruben Edward, was five years old. Ruben woke up a little late that morning, but moving as fast as he could, he rushed to get ready for school. Because it was a foggy morning, the bus driver did not see Ruben running from the house toward the bus stop and drove off without him. Ruben walked back home and since we had time to talk, he happily told me about a beautiful dream he had that night. Then he ran off to play with Ramiro who had just celebrated his second birthday three days before. A few hours later, Pat was ready to leave for work, but before leaving, the boys begged him for a little ride around the block in the pick-up truck. He agreed and they all climbed in and drove off.

I began to finish cleaning up the kitchen. Suddenly I heard a long screech and then a loud crash from the street and felt my heart sink. A dreadful feeling that something terrible had happened was confirmed when I saw Pat yelling and running down the street toward the house. At the intersection, a young and inexperienced driver ran the stop sign and came crashing into Pat's truck on the driver's side. The impact threw the passenger door open, throwing both children out of the truck and on to the street. As the truck continued to roll, it ran over both of them. The next thing I saw were the bodies of our two precious sons laying in the middle of the street, victims of a young and reckless young driver.

I'll never forget that saddest sight of my life. The ones we called our beloved boys, both gone from our life and from this earth – in an instant. Fifty years later, I wrote a poem about the dream Ruben described to me that morning.

Ruben's Dream

Mama, I had a beautiful dream,
My brother and I in a canoe,
Rowing along on a beautiful river,
With lots of flowers in bloom.

My sweet dear child
The grass on your grave,
For many years has been growing,
In this dream you saw your fate,
Like few men ever knowing.

Ramiro Israel (1 yr old) and Ruben Edward (4 yrs old)

The tragic death of our only two children, Ruben and Ramiro, was such a terrible blow. We could not forget them; we could not believe they were gone. Every time a door opened, we expected to see the children walk in. Everything reminded us of our precious ones and we wept for them incessantly. Every night our pillows were wet with tears. How we missed them. Yet the Lord had given me a sign that I was able to understand only after they were gone. Nine days before, I had seen a vision. In this vision, the Lord took me to a high hill and showed me the heavens. There I saw two parallel lights running across the sky. They traveled together from one side of the sky to the other, from sunrise to sunset. A voice told me to count the times they appeared, for they are the number of death. That number was nine. On the ninth time, at mid-sky, the two lights were cut off. I had interpreted that vision to mean that I was going to die in nine years. However, my interpretation was incorrect, for it was exactly nine days later, at mid-day that my sons were killed. As much as I wished that I could go back in time and change the events of that day, I knew that my vision and Ruben's dream meant that their deaths had been predestined. Therefore, I could never blame Pat for the accident and I kept him from blaming himself. Forgiveness was crucial to the preservation of our marriage. I knew that I was committed to my marriage for life.

We called on the Lord for consolation; but the tears continued to soak our pillows at night. Their voices, their laughter, their play, had all ended so suddenly. Where were their little questions and words of love? The house and everything in it brought back memories of our dear children. Finally, we accepted the fact that they were gone and it was just the two of us. We declared like Job, "The Lord gives and the Lord takes away. Let the name of the Lord be blessed." We were not mad at the Lord or our destiny; we just simply missed our boys so much. Patricio began to pray for another son. He promised the Lord that if God granted him his desire, he would dedicate his life to the service of the Lord. In later years, because of this trial, I was able to comfort mothers who had suffered the loss of a child and help them work through the grieving process.

Shortly after our great loss, there was a convention in Riverside, California. Groups of church members from all parts of the United States were going. Some members of our church were going and invited Pat and I. They knew we were grieving and they thought the trip might help. I later learned that one woman was so moved by our faith in the midst of our trial that she decided to receive the Lord as her Savior. She was baptized during the convention.

While at the convention, Pat's brother, Lupito, invited us to come to Yuma, Arizona, where he was now the pastor, to help out with the music ministry. We agreed and moved to Yuma. Shortly after arriving, we started to organize the youth group and formed a youth choir, teaching them how to read music and harmonize. Sister Carmen Granillo directed the choir and I played the piano. We even gave free piano and trumpet lessons to those who showed interest in learning. This brought in a renewed enthusiasm among the young people and several young men were baptized during our stay. We experienced renewed joy in our lives. I prayed for the Lord to continue to fill the void and remove the pain. Pat found a job at a service station in Yuma and after work we directed the music ministry together.

Pat and I remained in Yuma for six months, from December through the end of May. In June many of the young adults left for the summer to find jobs in California. Pat and I decided to travel and visit other Apostolic churches. We visited Los Angeles and El Paso, and then returned to our home in Mission. However, we still found it too painful to live there. We needed more time to heal.

The Lord was caring for us during that time and He put it on the heart of brother Eliezer and his wife, Margarita De Leon to invite us to come to Weslaco, Texas. The church in Weslaco had a small one-room house on the property which was unoccupied and we moved in.

While in Weslaco, I knew that a good way to share the gospel was through ministry to the children, so I proposed that we hold the first Apostolic Vacation Bible School. The classes were held at Templo La Hermosa which was spacious. Margarita and I invited the neighborhood children as well as those from the surrounding churches. On the last day of school, we had a program and many parents attended and heard the gospel.

That September while in Weslaco, the Lord blessed us with our third son. During the delivery, however, I was given too much ether and after the birth, the nurses were unable to wake me. During that time I dreamed that I was walking alone in an open and deserted place far away. There was no street, no grass or trees, only me walking away. Finally, after seven hours, I began to hear my mother's voice calling out my name, faintly at first, and then louder and louder, until I regained full consciousness. Once again, my days on earth had been extended.

When I awoke and saw my son, I rejoiced. Our prayer had been answered. With joy we received our new little one and we named him Ruben after our first son. What a blessing to have a child in our home again, one we could hold in our arms, close to our hearts and call our own; one who would call us "Mommy" and "Daddy." He was sweet and full of grace just like his brothers. We never wanted to hear him cry…it hurt too much. Friends and relatives sent gifts and we welcomed the restitution of a son. The world was bright again. We renewed our promise to serve the Lord the rest of our lives. We prayed that he too would live to minister the light of God.

Shortly after Ruben was born, my beloved Mama Severita suffered a heart attack. She needed someone to care for her because she lived with her daughter, Toñita, who was handicapped and could not provide the more strenuous type of care she now needed. Our house was in the process of being moved from Mission to an empty lot we had purchased in Edinburg. The home was lifted and set on a large flatbed with wheels. Two weeks later, when our house had been transported and set up, Mama Severita came to live with us. Toñita came as well and she did the cooking while I tended both my newborn and my grandmother. It really put a demand on my life, but I was willing to do it. My grandmother's health was stable for eight months. Then, unexpectedly, she had a second heart attack and it seemed like she had died. We called the doctor. I immediately knelt by her bed and holding her hand I prayed that God would not take her just yet. She had a blind daughter, (my Aunt Adela) living in Mexico who had made us promise to get her before her mother died. "Since I can't see her, I want to at least hear my mother's voice before she passes," Adela had said. The Lord heard my prayer and Mama Severita revived. We sent word to Adela to come as quickly as possible. She arrived the same day. The doctor told us that this heart attack would take her life. Mama Severita lived for one more week. During this time, people came and visited with her. One day, sister Ebelia came. My grandmother immediately introduced her to Adela. Ebelia was very impressed that the patient, not the caregivers, was the most attentive person in the room, making the introductions and complemented Mama Severita on her presence of mind. Mama Severita replied, "Yes, I am still here, but actually, I'm not here."

"How can you say that?" I asked.

"My body is here but I'm very, very far away. I'm not afraid to die. Death is only a step ahead." She then turned to the others in the room and said, "I want you to call an ambulance to take me to my home in Mission. I will go with the Lord from there. I don't want Beatrice to remember that I died in her home."

On the day she died, I was comforted by her words, "I am not afraid to die." For her burial, I dressed Mama Severita in a new dress I made for her. To me, she looked beautiful. Her spirit was free and there was no more pain.

One day several years after the death of our children, Pat arrived at home after work. I could tell by the distressed look on his face that there was something he had to tell me. He sat down and told me the story. On his drive home there was a car following closely behind him - someone in a big hurry. The road was narrow and curved with only one lane in each direction. Looking into his rear view mirror, Pat saw the driver and a child standing on the seat next to him with his arm around him. The driver was speeding up and moving to the left to pass Pat. A trailer truck was coming around the corner, visible to Pat, but not to the driver passing him. Pat veered quickly to the right as far as he could, endangering his own life and narrowly escaping the ditch, allowing the driver of the car to avoid a head-on collision while passing. Pat, who to his last days never forgot a face, told me that the driver was the young man, (now with a son of his own) who had accidentally killed our two sons. Pat told me that the first thought that came to his mind was, "Will this reckless man experience firsthand, the unspeakable sorrow of possibly losing the life of his son, or even his own?" Then immediately the response was, "No, I will do whatever I can to provide him and his son a way of escape, even by risking my own life." Praise the Spirit of Christ who fills us with His forgiving power!

Chapter 9

Our Ministry in Texas

For you are God's workmanship, created
in Christ Jesus for good works, which God
prepared in advance for us to do.

EPHESIANS 2:10

The believers in Mission had bought a property in Edinburg for a future church site. This property was adjacent to the empty lot that Pat and I purchased in Edinburg and where we had moved our house. We now needed the Lord to supply the means with which to erect a church building. Pat was ready to serve the Lord as he had promised. In Edinburg, Pat met Pastor Burkley, a member of the United Pentecostal Church, who agreed to let us use his building once a week to begin Spanish-speaking services.

We started meeting and Pat led the music worship with his trumpet and I played the piano. Soon, some Spanish speakers began to visit. Since both congregations were small, we also attended the English speaking worship services with Pastor Burkley. A young Mexican laborer started to hear the Word of God and began attending the meetings regularly. He was a well-educated musician by the name of Sabino Estrada and had been a band director in Mexico. With a piano player and two trumpet players (or one guitarist, since Pat knew how to play both), we began to make a joyful noise unto the Lord.

More Mexican migrant workers began to come to hear the Gospel of Jesus Christ and our hearts rejoiced. It was not long, however, before the enemy of God would try and disrupt our progress. Pastor Burkley approached Pat one day and informed him that we would no longer be able to use the building. One of the members, an influential woman who was a strong financial supporter, did not like to see the poor Mexicans in her midst. Pat and I bowed our knees in prayer and asked the Lord for a place of our own where we could present the gospel to the Mexican people with liberty.

There were in Edinburg three families who congregated in Mission. Among them was the Canales family. When we first arrived in Edinburg, they had opened up their home to us for meetings. We began to have home meetings there again. They had a three-bedroom home. Their family consisted of mother, father, six sons and three daughters. Our one-bedroom house was across the street from the Canales family. During the summer months, the Canales family with their six boys and the youngest daughter would travel to Central California to work in the fields leaving the two older daughters, Bellita and Dora, both in their twenties, at home. In the summer of 1949, while the girls were home alone, one of them left something on the stove and went off to work. Their house caught on fire. The neighbors called the fire department. I saw the fire and knew the girls were already gone to work. My first thought was the piano, the heart of our music for our home-church meetings. I ran and asked one of the firemen if he could possibly try and save the piano and told him exactly where it was located. I watched and waited and prayed. Finally, coming out from the smoke, the fireman appeared and they were carrying the piano, untouched by the fire.

After writing to the Canales family and telling them about the tragic fire, Sister Ebelia wrote back and said, "So Satan cannot rejoice in what he did to our home, take whatever lumber was not burnt and use it for framing a church building. Regarding the piano, I want to give it to you. You saved it; it is yours!" The Canales family decided to stay in California and eventually bought a home in Visalia. The older girls stayed in Texas and Bellita moved in with us for a short time.

Marcos Garcia, Pat's brother, organized believers who were available to work. We took each piece of lumber, removed the nails, and stacked it ready for reuse. The amount of lumber was sufficient to build the entire building. Marcos and his wife, Mela and their four children moved into our small two bedroom house while he helped build and supervise the construction. Mela and I prepared the food for the workers. When the construction was finished, I donated the piano that had been rescued from the fire. It was the first piece of furniture set up in the church building. Out of adversity had sprung triumph. We now needed something very important - chairs.

One day, Pat and I were driving to Mission to price some chairs. We had a flat tire along the way. Finding a service station, we pulled in. I took little Ruben out of the car and decided to walk around with him while Pat worked on the tire. Behind the service station building was a large stack of folding chairs. Just what we were looking for!

I asked the service station attendant about them and he said they belonged to Enrique Flores. I quickly recognized the name, since he had been our neighbor in Mission and I had been his son's teacher at the private school. I told the attendant why I was interested and he quickly called Enrique and handed me the phone. Enrique told me that he had just put new seats in a theater he owned and didn't know exactly what to do with the old ones, so he was storing them at the garage. I explained our need. Without hesitation, he said, "Take whatever you want and use them for your place of worship. You don't have to pay me anything." We lifted up our hearts in praise; God had provided. This was how the first Apostolic church was built and furnished in Edinburg.

During the time that we were working on the building, Pat and I had our fourth child. The circumstance of this birth was a great testimony of God's mercy. One evening in my seventh month, the doctor came by before he left on vacation to check on me. I had experienced a bit of back discomfort that day but I thought it was because I had helped Pat push the car that morning because it would not start. After checking my pulse, he said he wanted to examine me further. He immediately announced, "The baby is on its way, now!" Fifteen minutes later, I was holding my beautiful daughter. We named her Elizabeth. She was premature and weighed about five pounds. I had delivered her without pain. A Christian friend had told me that she herself had once given birth without pain and I had found it hard to believe, since I had experienced pain with all my other deliveries. But now, I believed.

A Caucasian neighbor, Mildred, came by to see my new baby and was quite surprised at how fair she was. Mildred said that none of her children was that fair at birth. My brother-in-law said Elizabeth was the most beautiful baby he had ever seen. I was so thrilled to finally have a girl and to me, Elizabeth was my little doll. Uncle Bennie and Tomasita had four beautiful daughters, my cousins Stella, Emma, Dahlia and Irma. I loved them very much and enjoyed combing their hair in French braids. I also had sewn many dresses for them. Now I could make dresses for my own baby girl.

One day, while the building was still under construction, the workers had left a ladder positioned to access the attic area. My sister-in-law, Mela and I had gone over to see if there was anything we could do to help. We were sitting and talking and I had my one-month old, Elizabeth, in my arms. I happened to look up and noticed my son Ruben, who was twenty-seven months old, walking on the twelve-inch plank that had been laid across the ceiling beams for access to the electrical wiring. My heart started thumping and I was filled with fear. "Oh Lord, please don't let my son fall," I prayed silently. I didn't scream or shout. I handed my baby over to Mela, walked over and climbed up the ladder. When I reached the top, I calmly called to Ruben, "Please walk slowly over to me." Without hesitation, he came to me as he usually did, but every step he took made my heart tremble. With thankfulness of heart, I praised God as I held him in my arms and carried him carefully down the ladder.

The Lord had gifted us with a building, a piano and chairs. Now we needed people to fill the building. One day, I felt inspired and decided to take a taxi to another neighborhood to speak to people about Jesus. I got out of the taxi, walked down the street, knocked on a door and introduced myself. I told the residents why I had come. They welcomed me and introduced themselves as the Revilla family. The mother was sick with boils and blisters all over her body. Her bed sheet was soaked with blood and pus from her sores and the prescribed medications were not helping her. I told her that that we believed in the power of prayer and that Jesus could heal her. I told her my husband and I would fast and pray for her. A few days later, while fasting and praying, Pat and I paid this family a visit. We witnessed to them of the Lord Jesus and then prayed earnestly for Mrs. Revilla and left. The next time we went to visit her, the sores were completely healed! The Lord had answered our prayers. The Revilla family fully acknowledged the miraculous healing work of God and started coming to our meetings. Not too long afterwards, ten members of the family surrendered their lives to Christ and were baptized. Others who heard their testimony also believed.

Pat met an English-speaking minister and asked him to support our ministry in Edinburg. Sam Pesnell and his family joined us. Pat asked him to take the lead in preaching the Word. A young Jewish man, whose last name was Diamond, was also converted to the Christian faith, and began to meet with us. Both he and Brother Pesnell preached to the Spanish congregation in English. Once again, my knowledge of both languages was useful as I was able to translate the sermons into Spanish. Here is an excerpt of a testimony written by Brother Sam Pesnell in the *El Heraldo Apostolico Editorial,* February 15, 1952.

> *Greetings in Jesus name: What a sweet fellowship we've had in the Rio Grande Valley with the blessed Saints of our Dear Lord Jesus. We have seen the real Power of the Day of Pentecost in our midst! We have been helping Brother and Sister Garcia in Edinburg, Texas. Sister Bellita Garcia has been teaching the Young People to sing in Spanish and English. And the Lord has manifested His grace and glory. Brother Patricio serves as pastor and what a blessing to work with him and his family! I*

have been preaching in English and Sister Garcia interprets the sermons into Spanish…Love and peace to all the Saints. Your Brother in Christ, Sam Pesnell.

Indeed, the Lord had blessed us. The Lord had provided the land, the wood, the builders, the chairs, the ministers, the interpreter, the piano and pianist, the trumpets and musicians, and now the new converts. There were great testimonies of healings and many were added to the church. Brother Gil Moreno, (who is now my pastor) his mother, Maria and sisters, Aurora and Rosie also came from Mission and supported us in the Lord's work in Edinburg.

Church in Edinburg 1953– (circled L to R) Bro. and Sis Revilla, Assistant Pastor Sam Pesnell and wife Ada, Pastor Patricio and Beatrice Garcia, Ruben and Elizabeth Garcia in front row

We were pastors in Edinburg from 1948 through 1953. In 1953, we decided to move to Los Angeles, California. My Uncle Bennie had moved to Los Angeles and had been elected Bishop President of the Apostolic Assembly. His pastoral home had a basement that was available to us. Pat and I left all our possessions in Edinburg and donated the land and house to the Assembly. We were able to leave the building to the incoming pastor and his family free of any debt.

Chapter 10

God's Provision

And my God will fill your every need according
to His riches, in glory, in Christ Jesus

PHILIPPIANS 4:13

O ur little family of four came to Los Angeles with very little money. Since I was in ill health after suffering a miscarriage in Texas, I went to see a doctor shortly after arriving. The doctor said it might be good for me to have another child, since this might help correct my problem. Not long afterward, we had another beautiful baby girl. Pat said that he had hoped it would be another boy, but forgot about that when he saw his beautiful Alicia Ruth.

The birth of my daughter Alice (as we now call her) was difficult and left me very weak. I had hemorrhaged during the birthing process and had lost much blood. My blood type was hard to match, so no transfusion was given. Although the doctor did not want to release me, I insisted that I wanted to go home. The night I got home I had a dream that I was coming into the Lord's presence. As I approached Him, I thought, "Are my children coming also?" He gave me a compassionate look, which told me that He would let me remain with my children.

Six weeks later, I had my checkup. When the doctor saw me, he apparently noticed something unusual because he made an appointment for me at the Cancer Clinic. That night I had extreme hemorrhaging and Pat rushed me to the emergency room. I felt extremely weak and the doctor estimated I had about one pint of blood left, yet, because of the dream I had, I was confident that I was not going to die. Although I did not know it at the time, we now believe that what I experienced is called placenta previa. In my case, part of the placenta had remained in my uterus after the birth. My mother, who had come from Mexico, stayed a year and nursed me back to health. The prayers of my husband, my mother, and many other believers and His merciful kindness allowed me to live to raise my children in the way of the Lord.

When we left Texas, Pat had a job which only paid him thirty-five dollars a week. In Los Angeles, Pat found a steady job working at a service station and his starting salary was one hundred thirty-five dollars a week. By Texas standards, this seemed like a fortune. Soon, we were able to rent our own apartment. One year later, Pat found a job as a driver for the Pico Wheel Service in downtown Los Angeles picking up and delivering wheels and tires. This physical exercise helped him develop large biceps, which the children always enjoy watching him flex. One day, Pat came home and told me that Chris Burdick, the owner, was looking for office help and that I should check it out. Alice was now two years old and I felt comfortable leaving her with a babysitter. I went in for an interview and I got the job immediately. Mr. Burdick said that I could start by answering the phone and he would show me how to do the bookkeeping later.

When our son, Ruben, was nine years old, he started working as a paperboy for the Los Angeles Harold Examiner. His employer picked him up early in the morning and drove while Ruben tossed the newspaper and completed his route before going to school. After school, he sold the paper on the street corner right in front of Pico Wheel, so we were able to observe his skillful salesmanship. With his first paycheck, he bought me a nice wristwatch. With future checks, he bought us a set of pots and pans making payments of one dollar and fifty cents a week. Ruben also bought a set of encyclopedia which helped our children complete many homework assignments. I believe these early years of business and sales training contributed to his professional success. Ruben is currently the District Director of the U.S. Small Business Administration in San Diego. In addition, and more importantly, Ruben and his wife Alma are committed to the work of the Lord and hold home meetings where they have seen the Lord do wonderful miracles.

Not long after starting at Pico Wheel, Mr. Burdick made me the office manager. We were the only wheel company in Los Angeles that repaired wire wheels. When I started, the shop mainly balanced and straightened them. One of the employees at Pico Wheel had a drinking problem. He disliked Pat because Pat disapproved of his drinking on the job and his vulgar language. This employee was very skilled in repairing wire wheels, so Mr. Burdick overlooked his problem. This employee complained about Pat and Mr. Burdick decided to let Pat go. By this time, Pat had worked for Mr. Burdick for seven years and I had worked six. I said, "I'm sorry Chris, but if Pat doesn't work here, I don't work here either. We will leave together." The following week he gave Pat his final check, and I asked him to make it my last one also. Mr. Burdick pleaded with me not to leave because he needed me; nevertheless, I said goodbye and we walked out together. I wasn't worried. I knew the Lord would open new doors and provide for all our needs.

The following Sunday evening, as we were driving home from church, we stopped at a red light. A large truck was stopped in front of us. We noticed that the truck's lift gate was up, and the back was stacked with boxes. When the light turned green, the truck took off and the top boxes began to rock with the movement of the truck. One of the boxes fell. Then another came tumbling down, onto the street right in front of our car. We honked our horn, but the truck kept on going unaware that he was losing his cargo. Since the large boxes were blocking the road, the kids darted out, picked them up, and put them in our car. Then we raced off in pursuit of the truck to try and return them. Just as we caught up with it, another box fell out. Again, Pat honked the horn and flashed his lights, but the truck kept on going. A red light slowed our pursuit and even though the kids tried to keep the truck in sight, eventually we had to give up the chase. At home to our great delight, we found that the boxes were filled with Kellogg's cereals. We had our choice of Frosted Flakes, Corn Flakes, Raisin Bran, Corn Pops, Mini Wheats and my favorite, Rice Krispies, for a very long time! The Lord was truly our provider.

Shortly afterwards, we were in an auto accident on the freeway. I was injured with whiplash. We received some money as a settlement, and Pat used it to open a service station in Hollywood. During this time, I found other temporary employment. One day, I was walking to the bank and passed the Pico Wheel Company. Mr.

Burdick saw me and called me into the office. He said that he desperately wanted me back. He was unhappy with the person he had hired as my replacement. He explained that his business was doing so poorly that he had just bounced a thirty-five dollar check. After hearing all this, I agreed to return to work for him. I'm not sure why I didn't negotiate for more money at that point. Maybe it was that I didn't realize then what an asset I was to the company. But the Lord interceded on my behalf and soon after I returned to work, a customer came into the shop and was impressed with how well I ran the business. He said he was looking for an office manager and thought I would be perfect. He said he would pay me fifty dollars a week more than Mr. Burdick was paying me. When I told Chris about this offer, he was very upset that his customer would try and steal me away. I was seriously considering the offer, so Chris offered to raise my salary by fifty dollars a week. Sometime later, Pat decided to close down his service station since it wasn't profitable, and Mr. Burdick took Pat back at Pico Wheel.

After my return, the business started to prosper. Chris added a new service; chrome plating wire wheels. I instituted other money making changes; dealing directly with Cadillac, repairing their defective wire wheels, hubs and rims and replacing any defective spokes with new ones. I also added the sale of top brand tires. Tuning and chrome plating wire wheels were interesting jobs. It required that the hub, rim and spokes all be disassembled. All these parts were then sent out for plating. When they came back, we had to reassemble them which meant putting each spoke back into the hub and the rim properly. This was called lacing. They were then placed on a spinning wheel for balancing. Finally, each spoke was tested for just the right sound with a small tuning tool. This process was called tuning the wheel.

Movie stars and television actors frequented our wheel shop since they owned the fine cars like Lamborghini, Mazarati, Mercedes, and Jaguars, which typically had chrome plated wire wheels. I did not go to movies or watch much TV, so I didn't recognize any of the actors. On one occasion, I told my boss's grandson, Gary, who was working at Pico Wheel that someone had come in who was very proud of his name. I told Gary that the man had told me three times that his name was Adam West. "Who is Adam West?" I asked. He told me that he was the actor who played "Batman" on the television series. When I went home that evening, I mentioned that I had met Adam West and my children were all excited because they knew who he was. This was how I also met John Wayne, Dean Martin, Ricardo Montalban, Linda Carter, Desi Arnez Jr., Sammy Davis Jr., Jerry Lewis, Karen Carpenter, Tony Dow, Steve McQueen, Sidney Poitier, and Charlton Heston. Whenever Gary told me that the person who drove in was a movie or TV star, I would call my daughter Alice to come to the shop to get their autographs. She was always very excited about the chance to meet a star. These celebrities always treated me kindly. Some brought me presents at Christmastime like boxes of candy and fruitcakes. Dean Martin gave me a leather brush kit embossed with his name, which I still have. The top of the brush has a zippered compartment that holds a comb, nail file and nail clipper.

My years at Pico Wheel were not without peril. There was a period when business was slow and Mr. Burdick, without my knowledge, had told Lionel, our newest employee, that this was going to be Lionel's last week. Mid-week, Lionel's brother showed up at closing time. In a very angry tone, he asked me why we were going to fire his brother. I told him that I did not know why and that I didn't make those decisions. The next thing I knew, he pushed his way into my office. I saw him raise his hand to strike me and I noticed a shiny object in his hand. I prayed, "My God, help me, this man is going to kill me!" I did not know what he had in his fist, but I thought it might be one of the hammers from the shop. He struck me on the head, and I went down. As he continued to hit me, he told me "Don't scream or I'll kill you." When he said that, I realized I was still alive and I could scream, and so I did. The men in the shop heard me and ran to my rescue. They pulled him off of me and restrained him. There on the office floor I saw the dented beer can he had used to hit me. The police came, and they asked me to go to the police precinct to file a complaint. I called my daughter Alice and asked her to meet me at the police station because I was still shaking after the attack. When she saw me, she pleaded with me not to go back to Pico Wheel. However, I did not want to let this man's actions disrupt my life. Mr. Burdick acknowledged my commitment to the success of his business and told me his plan was to someday give me a share of Pico Wheel Company.

Days later, Ramon Rios, the employee who came to my rescue, told me that Lionel's brother was upset because if Lionel lost his job he could no longer give him money – money which he needed to support his drug addiction. I was summoned to appear at the Los Angeles County Jail and identify the man that had attacked me. For his offense, the man received a short jail sentence. A few months after being released, he committed a horrible crime. In a fit of anger against his mother-in-law, he accidentally killed his wife as she tried to protect her mother. Once again, the Lord had delivered me. "No weapon formed against you shall prosper." Isaiah 54:17.

Chris Burdick retired and turned over the business to his grandson, Gary Stevens. When Gary was in a major motorcycle accident and out on disability, I had the responsibility of running the shop for many months by myself. During this time, I worked in the office and also supervised the shop. I worked for this company like a true business partner for a total of twenty-five years. Yet, in spite of what I had been told, I never received a share of the business. Regardless, I did not shy away from hard work and believed that we can do all things through Christ who strengthens us. Not only did I work full-time and raise my family, but I also actively served in the functions and leadership of the church.

In September of 1972, a newspaper reporter came in to service her car. She noticed that I was out in the shop showing one of the new workers how to lace the wheel. She was so impressed that a woman could do this type of work that she interviewed me and wrote a feature article which was published in the *Herald Examiner* on October 2, 1972.

Give the Little Lady

If She Isn't Fixing Wheels...

By CAMILLA SNYDER
Herald Examier Staff Writer

Smart members of the vroom, vroom set don't take chances with their wire wheels.

Whether one drives the tiniest Triumph or the loftiest, costliest Lamborghini, when you get 20,000 miles on your spokes, a visit to Beatrice Garcia is as important as a periodic visit to your dentist.

Who's Beatrice Garcia? And why take your wire wheel problems to a 58-year old housewife who can't drive a car and looks as if she should be busying herself with church work and PTA meetings?

Seventeen years ago, when her third child was a couple years old, Mrs. Garcia needed to supplement the family income. She had a next-door neighbor willing to care for her children but she wanted to work in the neighborhood. So she walked half a block down the street to the Pico Wheel Co., where her husband Pat worked. She asked owner Christopher Burdick for a job. He put Mrs. Garcia to work, and before he really realized what she was up to Mrs. Garcia was doing everything.

"I keep accounts payable, I keep accounts receivable, I answer the phone. I teach the boys how to change tires," Mrs. Garcia explains.

She's too modest to say she saves lives. That she can run her fingers quickly over a 72-spoke wire wheel, and tell you in the twinkling of an eye what the wheel needs.

"Sometimes they need tuning, sometimes they need to be laced up, sometimes they need chrome plating, sometimes they need to be torn down and reassembled," Beatrice Garcia says.

Christopher Burdick went into business in 1923 when most cars had spoke wheels-some wood, some wire, some steel. His firm today is said to be tops in the United States.

He and Mrs. Garcia, thanks to the vintage car craze, is seeing some 1923 wheels the second time round.

"There are two lives in wire wheels. I mean spoke wheels," Burdick says. "There is the original life of the wheel, then, if you have been at the Pomona Fair Grounds lately, you've seen the second life of the wheels on restored vintage automobiles.

"The cars belong to men who have made their fortunes, who have retired. Then the doctor says to them. 'Find something to do'. They go out and buy old cars and set about restoring them. We fix the wheels."

Mrs. Garcia's favorite story is about a doctor who drove his Jaguar through the shop door with the wheels wobbling.

"I said, 'Heavens your wheels are coming to pieces.' Fix them or you will be in trouble."

"When the doctor came back to get his wheels he brought his wife along to meet me. He said 'This is the lady who diagnosed the problem with my car.' I didn't know a lady could do that."

Mrs. Garcia didn't let the physician off with merely a repair bill.

"How about you helping me now?" she said. "I have just developed an ulcer."

The grateful physician recommended feeding the ulcer with milk. It worked.

Beatrice Garcia and Christopher Burdick have friends way beyond the Los Angeles area where they are situated.

"We get wire wheels in from New York, San Francisco, Minneapolis, Dallas, Chicago, and all over," Mrs. Garcia explained. "I guess some of them come from pretty important people. I never pay any attention to who they are. I just get the wheels in proper condition."

a Great Big Hand

That's no odd-looking mixing bowl Beatrice Garcia is whipping things up in. She's (believe it or not) repairing an automobile wheel.

Chapter 11

Continue to Witness

For God so loved the world that He gave his only Son, that whoever believes in Him shall not perish but have eternal life.

JOHN 3:16

In 1953, when we first arrived in California, we met with the Apostolic church in Mid-City Los Angeles. The building name was El Siloe. While serving as pastors in Texas, Pat and I had done much evangelizing in homes and we wanted to continue. With the permission of our pastor, Reverend Antonio Nava, we began leading small home meetings during the week with members who lived in Los Angeles, Torrance, and Culver City. They would invite neighbors and friends to come hear the gospel. Whenever there were new converts, we always took them to El Siloe for baptism. The congregation of El Siloe continued to grow, so they moved to a larger building in East Los Angeles.

In 1962, desiring to spread the gospel in our own neighborhood again, Pat found a church building to rent in Mid-City Los Angeles. Working with the Hispanic community, many received the Lord and asked to be baptized. Some went on to serve in full-time ministry in the Apostolic church.

The church had a women's auxiliary group, called the "Dorcas." The women in this group used their talents like cooking and making hand crafted items to do fund raisers. The profit was used to provide charity to those in need. The leadership team also organized weekend conferences and retreats, and many other things for spiritual edification. It was my privilege to serve as an officer in the Dorcas for many years in the following capacities:

1949-1951	Secretary – District of Southern Texas
1951-1953	Vice President – District of Southern Texas
1954-1956	Secretary – District of Southern California
1958-1962	Sub-Treasurer – National Ladies Auxiliary
1962-1964	Treasurer – National Ladies Auxiliary

In 1964, Uncle Bennie joined us as pastor of our small congregation in Mid-City Los Angeles with Pat as the assistant pastor. We evangelized by knocking on doors and praying for our contacts. The youth group increased and there were always young people over to our house visiting and in fellowship with our teenage children.

In 1965, shortly after his high school graduation and during the Vietnam War, our son, Ruben enlisted in the Army. After boot camp, he was nominated to go to West Point Preparatory School. After completing the training, instead of being deployed to Vietnam, he received orders to go to Germany. During Ruben's absence, we invited two young sisters, Raquel and Elisabeth Cervantes, to live with us since they were without family in Los Angeles. They became part of our family and loved us as much as we loved them. They are both married now and their children call me grandma.

The congregation was growing and praying for a larger building of our own. As treasurer, I knew we were in a position to offer a good down payment on a building. Pat and I began searching. While driving around in the Lincoln Heights area, Pat saw a building he liked. Although the church building had no "For Sale" sign, Pat stopped in front of the building and invited me to go in with him to inquire. We entered just as the board members were finishing up their monthly meeting. When we told them why we were there, they were surprised. They had just agreed on their plan to purchase another property with the intent to build a church on it. They told us that once the new building was completed, they would sell their present site. We immediately contacted Pastor Cantu. The building at 2450 Griffin Avenue was purchased one year later, in 1973 and is still there and currently being pastored by Val Jimenez and his wife Emma Cantu Jimenez. It was named Templo Emmanuel.

After Ruben returned from military service, he served under the mentoring of Pastor Cantu who ordained Ruben into the ministry some years later. During Ruben's first Sunday sermon, Alice, Tony, and three others accepted the Lord. They were baptized the following Sunday by Ruben. We were happy serving in the ministry at Templo Emmanuel, yet we were always open to the Lord's leading. One weekend in the summer of 1979, Pat and I went to a Christian retreat in the mountains. The last night we were there, the guest speaker preached from the book of Joshua, Chapter 14. This passage talks about the distribution of the land of Canaan to the children of Israel as their inheritance. In the passage, Caleb who was now eighty-five years of age, said to Joshua, "Today I am still as strong as I was on the day Moses sent me out (*to spy on the land*); as my strength was then, so my strength is now.... therefore give me this hill country." This hill country Moses had promised to him was the land that they had seen forty years earlier. Most of the men who had gone with Caleb came back and reported that there were "giants" in the land. Caleb and Joshua, on the other hand, were trusting in God that they would be able to subdue these "giants."

During the sermon, I felt the Lord's call to return to the Mid-City Los Angeles area to seek the lost souls. This area of Los Angeles was a very dangerous place because of the poverty, dropout rate, and crime. But I felt confident that, with the Lord on our side, we could overcome any obstacles or "giants." When we left the meeting, I asked Pat how he felt about that sermon. He said he felt the same way I did and that regardless of our age, we were still younger than Caleb was when he claimed the land. Many of our friends felt we were taking on a big challenge since Pat was now sixty-two and I was sixty-five. Most people our age were thinking about retirement. We spoke with Pastor Cantu and told him of our desire; he and the entire congregation of Emmanuel gave us their blessing. Pat was Assistant Pastor and I served as church treasurer and treasurer of the women's group at Templo Emmanuel until we left in 1979.

In Mid-City Los Angeles, we found a building to rent and had our first church meeting with our family and a few members from Templo Emmanuel who had come to support us. We were nine adults and three children, twelve in all, the perfect number since the Lord himself had twelve disciples. That same week we went door knocking in the neighborhood. The Cortez family opened their door to us. They had five daughters and they were more than happy to send the girls to Sunday-school. As the Cortez daughters got to know us better, their parents opened their home and hearts to us. Mrs. Cortez asked us to pray for her ulcerated leg since, due to some infection, the doctors said they would have to scrape it to the bone. Our prayers were answered and she received divine healing. Because of this, not only did the immediate family come to the Lord, but also many of their relatives.

On September 1, 1982, we purchased the site at 2330 Naomi Avenue, in Mid-City Los Angeles and named it South Central Apostolic Church. Pat, our son Ruben, and I ministered at this site for twelve years. During this time, Alice and Tony helped with the Sunday-school classes. Alice and others helped direct the children's youth, and adult choirs. I helped with the piano and was Treasurer. We made tamales and pies for fund raising. On holidays, we made turkey dinners and invited members and neighbors to come and eat freely. Everyone enjoyed the pumpkin and apple pies I made. Whenever the children needed tutoring, I would go with them into the dining area during the sermon and help them with their homework. Many of the children's parents only spoke Spanish, so the children needed extra help. I knew that these children would be the first in their families to graduate from high school, and I wanted to do everything possible to make this happen. To my knowledge, every single one of them graduated from high school and some went on to receive college diplomas.

Pat and I continued to work at Pico Wheel while serving as pastors of our congregation. Our service to the body of Christ was done with all our heart, our soul and our strength. We believe the Lord will reward us in that day.

One winter morning in 1980, I began to feel very sick at work. I had never experienced such a severe headache. Pat rushed me to the hospital where they determined that I was experiencing a stroke. I was admitted to the hospital, and although coherent, I barely remember what happened the next three days. I told Pat that perhaps it was my time to go. He gently placed his arm around me and said, "No, you can't go, I cannot live without you. I have already asked the Lord to take me first." He began to pray. I knew my husband loved me, but it was that day I understood how deeply. I prayed that God would allow me to stay by my husband's side a bit longer. I recovered and years later, as he had requested, Pat went on to be with the Lord first at the age of eighty-eight.

On the day I had the stroke, I was admitted into the Intensive Care Unit of the California Hospital in Los Angeles. We were advised that the chances were very high that I would have a second and more severe stroke, so they recommended surgery before that happened. My husband, family and church members all prayed. After we prayed, we felt led to refuse the surgery and decided to wait on the Lord. The first few weeks my condition was unstable. No one was permitted to visit except my immediate family. One day, Pat came to visit and asked if our daughters had come that day. I answered that no one had come except the "Brother" who had come to pray with me. Pat asked me which brother had come. I said, "The one dressed in white, who left as you came in. Didn't you see him?" He had not seen anyone go out the door, but thought that the person must have been a doctor.

On another occasion, when Alice was visiting me, I told her that the Brother was standing right beside her. She looked around and saw no one but said nothing to me. I told her that the Brother came every day to teach me beautiful psalms. I asked her if she would like to hear the one he was teaching me now and she said she would. Alice told me later that they were the most beautiful psalms she had ever heard. She asked the doctor if they had prescribed any medication that might be causing me to hallucinate. They told her that they were not giving me anything that would have such side effects. I continued to recite the words I learned from the Brother, words that filled me with joy and peace.

Several Charismatic (Spirit filled) Catholic student nurses enjoyed visiting me every day to hear me recite the psalms I was learning. One day, I had a very high fever, and the head nurse said, "Mrs. Garcia, the doctor has tried everything and your fever will not go down."

"Do you mean only God is able?" I asked.

She said "Absolutely."

When the student nurses came in, I asked them to pray with me. Within the hour, my temperature had dropped and the fever was gone. The nurses began to thank God for He had answered our prayers.

My health continued to improve daily and I was recovering the use of my right side. I was now walking around the hospital hallways using the handrail. One day, Alice was visiting and I said, "Here comes the Brother." She told me that she didn't see anyone and asked me to describe him. I replied, "He's in his mid-thirties, has an oval face and is wearing a three-piece brown suit." I was just about to describe his eyes, when I saw the Brother shake his head. "Alice, I cannot describe him to you any further," I said. This was the last time the Brother came to visit me. After leaving the hospital, I wished I could see the Brother again. I believe someday I will. I know that God is my heavenly Father because I have been born again into His family. Jesus said, "For whoever does the will of My Father who is in the heavens, he is My brother and sister and mother." Matthew 12:50.

After six weeks in the hospital and shortly after my return home, we were notified by our landlords that the building had been sold and we would have to move out. During this time, my daughter Elizabeth and her husband were purchasing a house in La Mirada, California which was near La Habra, where my son Ruben and his family lived. We moved in with Elizabeth and Ralph who had three children, Stephen, Trisha, and David. Ruben and Patricia had two sons, Edward and Timothy. At that time, Alice and Tony had three children, Rick, Alan and Leslie and lived in Los Angeles near Montebello. I believe the Lord worked all this out for us to be close together. Elizabeth was home with me for a year and I had fully recovered by the time she found a full-time job. She went to work while I stayed home with my grandchildren. Stephen and Trisha went to the elementary school across the street and David, who was now age four, was my companion during the day. The children always enjoyed my cooking. Steven helped me in the kitchen to make enchiladas, mashed potatoes, and pumpkin pies. Trisha always helped me with the dishes. I enjoyed sewing pretty dresses for Trisha. Pat and I enjoyed living with them for five years.

In 1986, we moved from La Mirada and rented a duplex in Los Angeles. The duplex apartment was right across the street from my daughter Alice and her family. Tony and Alice had just had their fourth child, Kristy, and we wanted to be near them to help with our grandchildren. Pat and I would drive the children to school and after school I give them piano lessons. I had fun making Leslie and Kristy pretty dresses. We were so blessed to have lived across the street from Alice, Tony and our grandchildren for fourteen years.

During the time we lived there, I became good friends with our landlords, Aaron and Myrtle Rosenzweig. Myrtle promised me that Pat and I could live there as long as we wanted. When the renter in the second duplex apartment moved out, the Rosenzweig's rented it to us and we were happy to have it. Because of this, we were able to give hospitality to family and acquaintances on short visits to California. In addition, some of our grandsons lived in that second apartment when they needed to. In 1995, Myrtle passed away and Aaron decided to sell the duplex. Honoring his wife's promise, he gave Pat and me first option to buy the property. Since we were now both in our eighties, we didn't think we would qualify for a thirty-year loan at our age. Aaron agreed to sell us the property slightly below the market value price and we qualified! The building had two apartment units. Each unit had one bedroom, a bath, a kitchen and living room. This was a real blessing to us.

Since we lived so close to my daughter, we visited daily. Alice and I had signed up as a team for the church kitchen commission, which meant we would cook together once a month and sell the food after Sunday-school to raise funds. On one particular Sunday morning, we were preparing burritos and pumpkin pies. We had just finished and I was resting at the kitchen table. After tasting a burrito, Alice said, "These burritos are fit for a king." No sooner had she said it when there was a knock at the kitchen side door. Standing there was a well-dressed man of about thirty. He said, "Do you have anything to eat?" Alice felt an unexplainable joy at that question because she knew we had prepared something special and she wanted to share it. Without hesitation, she packed him a lunch with not just one, but two burritos, a piece of pumpkin pie, and a soda. He thanked her, took the bag, and she closed the door. Wondering why my daughter was so compelled to give a perfect stranger part of our church profit, I wanted to see who this person was. I looked out the kitchen window knowing that he would have to pass by to get to the sidewalk, but he never did.

"Alice," I said, "Who was it? I haven't seen anyone pass by." She was puzzled too. Perhaps he had gone into her backyard to eat the lunch. We checked the back yard but he wasn't there and there was no exit that way. We walked to the front looking up and down the street. The man had disappeared just as fast as he had appeared at the door. Who was this mysterious visitor? We may not know in this life, but we believe God's word, which says, "Do not forget hospitality, for through this some, without knowing it, have entertained angels." Hebrews 13:2.

One summer, when Pat and I were thinking about retiring as pastors, we decided to take a trip to Texas. Pat loved Texas and always talked about moving back there some day. We decided to take a train for a change and planned to visit several different places. We visited Corpus Christi, Houston, and finally, San Antonio where we attended a church convention. We saw many of our relatives and dear friends and had a wonderful time.

The train ride back home took about three days and we were just reaching the outskirts of Los Angeles when something happened. Pat and I were in the last car, which was the dining car, and had just finished a late breakfast when we heard and felt a jolting thump. "Oh my Lord," I said to Pat, "I think the train ran over a cow!" The dining car began rattling loudly and started rocking from side to side. The car was empty except for a young boy, Pat, and me. We started running, the boy first, with us close behind. Pat jumped over the coupling between the cars and reached back to pull me from the diner into the next car. Just after I jumped from one car to another, we heard a loud screeching and then stood there in shock as we watched the dining car go off the tracks. Suddenly, the train stopped moving. Then the lights and air conditioning turned off. As we looked back, we saw the diner had completely derailed; it was leaning on its side and across the tracks, forming a number seven. The car we were in was also leaning but still on the tracks. We were told to remain in the train until the ambulance came. It was a very hot day and the air inside the train was suffocating. It took two hours to detach the derailed diner.

After a while, people started to calm down and I took a seat. I heard the woman sitting next to me weeping. I asked her if she was OK. She told me that she had been on another train earlier that morning which had also derailed. The passengers from that train had been transferred to our train in El Paso. She could not believe that something like this could happen twice in one day! She feared this was a result of some curse or bad luck following her. I asked if she or anyone in that first train accident had been hurt and she said "No." Then I said to her that maybe she was looking at it from the wrong perspective. In my thinking, surely what she had experienced this day was God's bountiful mercy. Perhaps instead of weeping, she should be praising the Lord for saving her from the same mishap not only once, but twice in the same day. She then calmed down and thanked God. We arrived home, a little late and tired, but thanking the Lord for His protection.

A very special day in our married lives together was in 1990 when we celebrated our 50th wedding anniversary. Pat and I renewed our wedding vows and my Uncle Bennie officiated at the ceremony and reception. My mother, who was ninety-five years old, came from Mexico to join the celebration. It was a memorable event.

Chapter 12

Celebrating Healings and Blessings

"And let us not lose heart in doing what is good, for in the proper season we will reap if we do not faint."

GALATIANS 6:9

In March of 1992, Pat and I retired as pastors of South Central after twelve years and once again, surrendered the building to the Apostolic Assembly, fully paid. Although retired, Pat and I continued to help the new pastor, Jorge Solis and his wife Becky, as assistant pastor and superintendent of the Sunday-school classes. In 1996, Brother Andres Mayoral and his wife Ruth became the new pastors, and we continued to help until 2000. When Pat was eighty-one years old, he baptized his grandson, Alan Landeros. In addition to the five years of ministry in Texas, we labored a total of forty years in the Mid-City area of Los Angeles. Evangelism and care for the body of Christ were the focus and joy of our lives.

It was in his early 80's that Pat started to show symptoms of Parkinson's and dementia, and his condition was slowly impacting our lives. Pat began to have difficulty staying awake while driving. He often fell asleep at stoplights. One day we had gone to the store and Pat decided he would stay in the van and sleep a bit while I went in and bought the things we needed. This time, for some reason, he could not sleep and decided to go find me in the store. As he was approaching the store, someone coming out pointed and said, "Look at that van, it's on fire!" For some reason, our van had caught on fire, but my dear Pat was not in it. We found out later that there was an electrical short in the engine and the insurance company classified the van "totaled." Pat stopped driving about six months later.

In October of 1999, Alice and her family moved from Los Angeles to Placentia in Orange County. Pat and I rented out our duplex and moved into their Los Angeles house with our granddaughter Kristy and grandson Alan, who had stayed so they could finish the school year. Alan willingly helped me with Pat and shared with the responsibilities as Pat's caregiver. After a year, Pat and I and Alan and Kristy moved to Placentia to live with Tony and Alice in their new home. Both Alice and Pat and I eventually sold our properties in Los Angeles.

On May 6, 2000, Pat and I celebrated our 60th wedding anniversary at the Montebello Quiet Cannon Country Club. At this celebration, Pat stood up and quoted Proverb 31, which asks, "A virtuous woman, who shall find her?" Pat said, "I have!" Then I spoke and said that I too had been blessed with a man who had always shown me great love and patience.

On May 12, 2005, we celebrated our 65th anniversary at a nice restaurant with friends and family. Pat was always my true companion.

We did everything together, especially pray. Pat was a faithful and loving husband; a quiet man who loved my cooking and never forgot to compliment me. He especially loved my apple pies and always said they were the best.

After moving to Placentia, we registered Pat with the Easter Seals Adult Day Care Center in Brea. He would go several hours daily. It helped him to have activities to stimulate his mind. Our special outing, of course, was Sunday morning worship service.

One day while at home, Pat fell and broke his hip. He came home three weeks after his surgery. The following morning was September 11, 2001 and while preparing breakfast we turned on the TV to watch the morning news. We were shocked to hear that four commercial passenger jet airliners had been hijacked by terrorists. One of the planes had intentionally crashed into one of the Twin Towers of the World Trade Center in New York City. The top of the building was engulfed in flames. As we watched in shock, we saw the second tower hit by another jet airliner. We began to pray. In the following months, we saw renewed patriotism as American flags were displayed everywhere and neighbors began to talk to one another and build new friendships out of their need for comfort and security.

After surgery, Pat had difficulty walking. I would push him around the block in his wheelchair. Sometimes, to encourage him to walk, I would have him push me for a short distance on the way back. One of our neighbors, Stephanie Leon, who often did gardening in her front yard, noticed us. She was confused and came over to ask who was supposed to be in the wheelchair, me or Pat. We got a laugh out of that! This is how I met Stephanie who became a dear friend.

We cared for Pat at home but eventually realized he needed to be in a homecare facility. We found one nearby. After suffering a stroke which took away his capacity to swallow, Pat went to stay in a nursing facility where we visited him every day. In the last week of his earthly life, Pat did not speak, but on the day before he died, we clearly heard him ask, "Where is my wife?" I went to his side and held his hand. My beloved Pat went to be with the Lord on September 25, 2005. After my dear husband's passing, I went to live with my daughter, Elizabeth and her second husband, Ron Martin.

I have been on several vacations with Ron and Elizabeth which I have enjoyed very much. I went with them to Sedona, Arizona for a week. Our trip to Sedona included a stop in Portal, Arizona at Ron's cousin's house. We stayed overnight and Vicki's husband, Rick showed us the observatory built over his garage. The sky was amazingly clear, and through the telescope, I saw some of the stars shine with beautiful colors. It was a magnificent sight which I will never forget. We continued to Sedona and had a wonderful time there.

The following year, Ron and Elizabeth were going to Flagstaff, Arizona, and Alice and I joined them. While there, we took a day trip to Sedona. We went to a popular restaurant in town for a late breakfast. The line was long and many people were waiting outside. As we waited, a gentleman introduced himself. He said he was an Inca Indian. I told him about my American Indian ancestry. Eventually, I asked him if he believed in the Lord Jesus, and he said he had his own beliefs. I mentioned that I had just read a book called *The Peace Child* about a missionary and his wife who went to share the gospel of Jesus Christ with some Inca Indians in Peru. The missionary had taken food and many gifts to them. The tribe had been at war with its neighboring tribe for many years. They continued fighting even during the months he preached to them about peace. Feeling discouraged, the missionary and his wife decided to leave. The tribal leaders begged him to stay and promised they would make peace between the two villages.

The next day the chiefs from both villages arrived in front of the missionary's house, each holding a baby in his arms. With words of promise, the two chiefs exchanged babies. Each child would forever be called "The Peace Child." Each would live as a member of the other tribe, so that if anyone from either side sought war, he would be attacking his own child. The missionary asked the chiefs if there was any other way to make peace, without the pain of giving up a child. They assured him that, for them, there was no other way. He asked them how they chose whose baby would be given up. The two chiefs looked at him and said, "Why, we gave up our own sons, of course!" At that moment, the missionary realized the significance of this exchange. He told the chiefs, "That is the very same thing that God has done in Jesus Christ! God gave his only Son!" The missionary opened up his Bible and read to them from Isaiah 9:6. "For unto us a child is born, a son is given... And He shall be called, Wonderful Counselor, Mighty God, and Prince of Peace." For the first time, the tribes began to understand the message of Christ.

"My friend," I told him, "The Lord Jesus Christ is our Peace Child." His heart was so touched by this story that he said he now believed. His ten-year-old daughter, who was standing nearby as we spoke, was listening attentively. I pray that the seed of salvation was planted in her heart, too. As our name was called to dine, we said, "Goodbye." He gave me a hug and said "God bless you my little sister." I felt joy for the opportunity to encourage someone to become a child of God.

Speaking about children, I feel very blessed to have great-grandchildren. My granddaughter Trisha and her husband Rudy have four children, so I have had the joy of watching my precious great-grandchildren Jake, Allison, Katlyn, and Kimberly grow up. For my ninety-fourth birthday, Trisha and Rudy prepared a wonderful party for me in their home. I will always treasure the memory of getting together with so many friends and family on that special day.

I have enjoyed happiness and peace, living with Ron and Elizabeth. Ron welcomed me into their home as if I were his own mother. I have met some of the neighbors who have become my friends and for whom I am praying. Elizabeth and I read the Bible in the morning which keeps us strong in the faith. We also have a small home Bible group with whom we have fellowship during the week. Ron reads the scriptures to us after dinner which I enjoy very much.

I still feel great joy when I can help others. One day in September of 2003, while eating lunch at the Placentia Senior Center, I decided to walk to the store, one short block away. When I got there, I noticed a crowd. There was a man who was trying to get the group's attention, but no one was listening. He was asking them to form a line since he was going to distribute boxes of food. He had brought the boxes and bags of food in his big truck. He set up large tables in an empty parking lot on the corner of Bradford and Santa Fe Street. I went up to him and told him that no one was listening because he was speaking English and they only understood Spanish.

The man introduced himself to me as "Larry the Street Preacher." Larry asked if I would interpret. I was so glad to be of help. As soon as I gave the crowd instructions in Spanish, they formed a line. He then asked me to translate his message and prayer, which I did joyfully. Again being bi-lingual was useful. That same day, I met Dr. Minda Sena who was at the distribution center with her mother. They are both dear believers in Christ. After becoming good friends, Minda and I prayed about starting a Bible study at the Placentia Senior Center. Minda went to City Hall and obtained a permit granting us permission to do this. We held studies at the center for three years. I pray that the Word of God that was spoken will bear much fruit in the hearts of those who listened.

In January of 2004, while at the Senior Center, a lady said I was beautiful. I replied, "Oh no, I am not beautiful, you are." She spoke strongly to me and said that I should not deny the beauty of the Lord that others see in me. The next morning, I woke up with a poem in my head and I wrote it down. The poem first came to me in Spanish and then later my daughter, Elizabeth, helped me translate the poem into English. My poem was not only published in the International Who's Who in Poetry Book, but also received the Editor's Choice Award and was featured as the very first poem in the book. This was indeed a special award for me and a confirmation from the Lord that we are beautiful because of Him! I pray that others who read this poem might also recognize how beautiful we all are to our Creator.

Loved By the Creator

You were skillfully formed for a purpose,
For the honor, and glory of God.
You are the precious and loving perfection,
Of the beautiful plan of the Lord.

Oh, the workmanship of His hand, don't despise it,
With delight, He formed you in the womb.
You are loved and most precious before Him,
By the One, who was raised from the tomb.

He determined the place of your dwelling,
He selected your family, your race.
In His wisdom He fashioned your future,
Then led you by His mercy and grace.

He has shaped you through trials and sufferings,
In all these He partook of your pain.
And by these He was able to mold you,
Like the potter, molds clay in the flame.

So today you are how He made you,
With great love, He determined your fate.
So give praise to the hands of the potter,
Through your life shines Christ's glory and grace.

I was selected to represent the Placentia Senior Center in the 2010 Heritage Festival Parade.

Beatrice Representing the Senior Center in the Heritage Festival Parade in Placentia, California

Throughout my life, I've had many physicians, but it is really the Lord who has always healed me. To recount all his healings would be more than I could tell in this autobiography. I will, however, mention some recent episodes as a testimony to His healing power. In April of 2007, I went to Whittier Community Hospital with severe pain on my right side of the stomach. After an ultrasound, they discovered that I had gallstones. The attending doctor said I should have my gallbladder removed. The next day the surgeon came by and explained that the surgery was rather simple, and he would like to schedule it. I mentioned that I was ninety-three, and he replied that he had done surgery on patients my age before. I ask him how many of them had lived after the surgery. He did not reply. I refused the surgery. They sent me home with medication, which I had to discontinue because of side-effects. I watched my diet and went through a period of yellow jaundice. One night while I was praying, I heard the Lord say, "You are healed!" and I believed. From that day on, I had no more pain. Gradually I began eating regular meals again.

On October 31, 2007, I woke up in the middle of the night coughing up blood. Ron and Elizabeth rushed me to the Whittier Community Hospital. Although I was concerned, I was feeling reasonably peaceful. While Elizabeth was nervously negotiating with the emergency staff to administer some treatment for me, I said, "Lord, if this is the way You are going to take me, then I thank You for taking me without any pain." In my mind, I heard God say to me, "I'm not taking you yet." I was admitted that night and they put me on antibiotics. The next day, I was coughing up less blood. That day they performed a battery of tests and performed a bronchoscope to check my lungs. They found nothing to report. The attending physician reviewed my medical records from my last hospital visit.

He told me that this time, they should do the gallbladder surgery. I told him that Jesus is able to heal. Alice asked if they would first do an MRI to check on the condition of my gallbladder since six months had passed and I no longer had any pain. He agreed and scheduled the exam for that day. The next day, Julie Kazarian, who works at the hospital and is one of Alice's dear friends from church, as well as my grandson Alan, were visiting me when the doctor came in. He had already reviewed the results of the MRI and said, "Mrs. Garcia, I believe your God has healed you. You do not need surgery." We all began to praise God for his goodness!

At my ninety-fifth birthday we had seventy-seven guests. Many had been members of our congregation, and they spoke very kind words about Pat and me. Here are some of their testimonies:

Susan Cortez Lara recalled the many evenings during church services that I spent helping her with her homework. She said that, as the first in her household to graduate from college, she wished to share with me the honor of her Master's degree.

Nicolas Cortez (Susan's father) said the Lord had sent us into their neighborhood to bring them out of darkness into the light of Jesus. He said that everyone in his family felt like we were angels that had been sent to them.

Olivia Rubio said that when we first came to their door, she thought, "What in the world are these two little old people doing here?" She did not want to hear the gospel, but we did not give up. We continued to visit them until the entire family received the message of salvation. They were thankful that we were always there to pray and be with them in time of need.

Nora Martinez testified that after meeting and speaking with me, she had been comforted regarding the recent accidental death of her 5-year-old daughter. She realized her need to press forward and focus on the care of her two remaining children. After speaking, Nora had the opportunity to pray with my son, Ruben and Alma and received the Lord as her personal Savior.

After hearing there testimonies, I realized that Pat and I had done the right thing when we went back in to Mid-City Los Angeles to search for the lost souls and bring them to the light of Jesus Christ. We were constant in prayer for those whom the Lord had committed to our care.

Something we have enjoyed doing the past two years is celebrating Passover with our Jewish friends, Stephanie and Burke Leon. The ceremony includes the reciting of the Haggadah, which tells the story about the night God delivered the Hebrews from slavery in Egypt. It also includes the Seder meal, which consists of a lamb shank dinner (wonderfully prepared by Alice) with matzo soup and the bitter herbs for the Seder plate (prepared by Stephanie). I really enjoyed this ceremony and it was very special to hear Stephanie recite in Hebrew as we read along in English. I contributed to the celebration by telling the Biblical story of Passover and how the blood of the Passover lamb represents the blood that Jesus shed for us, so that we might also be saved. It was an honor to celebrate both the Jewish and Christian traditions as one.

My ninety-sixth birthday was very memorable. It was held in a mansion with friends and family members attending. This spacious Casa Blanca Mansion is located at the top of a hill in Orange,

California. It is owned by Stephanie Leon's son, Andrew. Stephanie and Andrew gifted it for our use on my birthday.

Because I have believed in Christ the King, I enjoyed the event at the mansion as a reminder that I am a child of God's Royal Family. I know that one day I will inherit an Eternal Kingdom. Thanks to Stephanie and her family for making this a memorable birthday.

96th Birthday

Epilogue

Many years have passed since my life first started. I have seen many changes in all areas of life. Things I never imagined are being done today. The new discoveries in science and technologies I may never understand. I realize that as Job stated, we come naked into the world and leave in the same fashion. So what will endure? What will remain of my life on earth? I hope my descendants will have treasured memories of me, and the love I shared with family, friends, and brethren in Christ. The love of God that I freely received, I have given to others. I have ministered that which I have received. I will praise the Lord with every breath that I take. By his mercy what we have sown in shame, we will reap in glory. There are many other marvelous ways in which the Lord has revealed Himself to me in my life. It would take many more pages to recount them all. I believe that for all those who love Him, and love his appearing, we will have eternity to recount the stories of His exceeding greatness toward us.

About the Author

M other was a voice of someone from "the Greatest Generation" who lived from 1914 – 2011. She was not rich or famous, although she met many who were. She was simply Beatrice Garcia, a Mexican-American woman rich in life experiences and blessed with the intelligence and mental capacity and wit to write and finish telling her life story at the age of 96.

Mother had a certain way of telling her stories that captured your attention and transported you to that time and space. Whether it was from her storehouse of personal experiences or a Bible story, she took you there and as she spoke it, you lived it.

Her book unveils the life of a resourceful fatherless girl that learns early on that life's adversities can become opportunities and paths to knowing the power of Christ's love. The courage of her youth, the proving of her faith, and her wisdom and steadfast commitment to the gospel of Jesus Christ, are revealed in this autobiography.

The last 6 years of her life, Beatrice lived with me, Elizabeth Martin, her oldest daughter, and my husband Ron in Fullerton, California. During this time, my sister Alice Landeros and I were able to capture all the final stories of her life and complete her autobiography. One week before her passing, on July 31, 2011, she had the joy of knowing that we had just completed translating her book *The Strings of My Heart* to Spanish, *Las Notas De Mi Corazon*.